Airborne

Getting your faith off the ground

Jose Zayas

Airborne

Getting your faith off the ground

Jose Zayas

CHRISTIAN
FOCUS

Contents

This book is dedicated to my wife, Carmen.
You are my forever love and closest friend.
My greatest joy is walking through life with you.
Thanks for believing in me!

To my son, Jonah.
You've taught me so much about God's love!
Daddy may travel a lot,
but know that you are in my heart
wherever I may be.
I love you!

Acknowledgements

Write a book and you'll learn about yourself. Though I hammered out the pages on my laptop, I'm forever indebted to family and friends who made this final manuscript possible. You'll find a lot of "family stories" in *Airborne*. My mom and dad, Miguel and Rosa, modeled for me what it means to follow Jesus in both the good and bad times. Thank you for everything ... and I mean everything!

To my brothers, Miguel and Rafael, and my sister, Raquel, for putting up with me! Your lives continue to challenge and inspire me.

To my mentor and friend, Dr. Luis Palau, for giving me the chance to serve and see evangelism "at its best." Luis, you are an inspiration! You have poured out your life into mine. I just hope that I will "pass it on" to the next generation.

To the Jose Zayas Evangelism International (JZEI) board of directors and ministry partners for freeing me up to travel and write. Special thanks to Mark and Tracy Martinez for pushing me to "sit down and write."

To my new friends at Christian Focus Publications for working so hard to get this published in record time!

To the team of professionals that helped shape the content of this book. To David Sanford, a caring agent who believed in this project from day one. To Mike Umlandt and Lissa Halls Johnson and others who edited each page with care. What would I do without you?!

To Dave Lubben, Greg Stier, and John Garrick ... friends and "like-minded brothers" who challenged my thinking and encouraged me to "finish strong."

To my loving Leader, Jesus Christ. You've rescued my soul and made life worth living. Please take these words and draw people to follow You!

Introduction

Airplanes, Adventures, and Jesus?

You're bound to meet a lot of people when you fly 100,000 miles a year.

I know. Because that's my story.

I'm a follower of Jesus Christ, and the reality of His work in my life has compelled me to share my experience with anyone willing to listen. Crossing countries and continents, I've dedicated my life to helping people take the first steps to experience radical personal change.

It can be difficult to thoroughly explain to the people I meet the deep mystery and joy of how they can know their Creator in a personal way. I've found that illustrations often communicate something my explaining cannot.

Jesus used word pictures much of the time to share truth. He told a group of farmers that the realm of God is like "a mustard seed" (Matt. 13:31-32). Jesus said that this tiny mustard seed would grow into a tree large enough to house a flock of birds.

What truth was He sharing? That His actions would transform tens of millions of lives for centuries. His message would grow. The farmers got the point; they saw it. I've chosen the analogy of a plane ride for this book as a way of explaining the adventure of following Jesus. Why a plane ride? Because plane rides have take-offs, landings, turbulence, and often involve conversations with all sorts of interesting people. Traveling by plane can illustrate the process of a relationship with Jesus Christ. This relationship is about a journey, not just an event or one moment in time. Following Jesus is supposed to be an adventure, a life's pursuit. Too often, the idea many people have about Christianity is of a Sunday event, where you go to a building and pay your dues to God. Not so. The Christian faith is meant to be more than a one-time encounter, much more than a religious exercise. It's a continual journey, taking you to places you've never seen and possibly haven't even dreamed about.

A plane ride is an ordinary yet out-of-this-world amazing adventure. Just look out the window from 35,000 feet in the air and you'll know what I mean. You can breathe, walk, talk on the phone, listen to music, watch a movie, or eat a meal while flying in a plane. That's ordinary life occurring while defying gravity!

The same can be said about following Jesus. Your life is filled with housework, stressful jobs, relationship challenges, and the stuff that makes the day-to-day seem ordinary. Yet followers of Jesus tackle life's challenges with the active intervention of God. That's what I call defying gravity. Read the Bible, and you discover the life stories of real people who also interacted with God. You'll find sex, drugs, witchcraft, love, and murder. There are villains and heroes, tearjerkers and happily-ever-after endings.

How do you explain God? He's so huge, so vast ... by His very nature He's above and beyond our comprehension. Yet we can know Him. Sitting in a brand-new Boeing 777 airplane helps me understand this. Huge engines are attached to the wings. There are miles and miles of wiring and computers with complex programs to make it all work. I just don't fully understand how a plane works. But I know that it does. That's the dynamic tension that you find in pursuing God. Yes, He's beyond your understanding. But you can know and follow Him.

A plane ride is about getting passengers to where they need to be. Pick up the Bible and you'll find that same theme from cover to cover. It starts with God shaping the universe by His very words and carving out the perfect garden for men and women to live in. Flip to the end and you're left with a graphic description of God's ultimate destination for those He loves – a heavenly paradise.

What's in the middle? The story of God. You get to look at how God has dealt with various types of people – young and old, rich and poor, genius and simple. Each encounter is different, yet the theme remains the same. God is looking to repair the damage of bad choices; He invades history and intersects people's lives. God wants to take us on a special journey.

My Brother's Story

Even though I travel all around the world sharing God's message of hope, my own brother Rafael didn't want anything to do with it. I know what it's like to watch

11

a family member miss out on such a great thing and remember agonizing times of frustration – not knowing what to say or how to say it!

For years, Rafael refused to go past the surface when it came to conversations about God or Jesus. He was quite happy living for himself and enjoying all of life's pleasures. Rafael didn't spend time thinking about consequences or evaluating his behavior. He was satisfied jumping from one party to the next.

Like many Americans, Rafael had seen his share of hypocrites acting "in the name of Jesus." He had read about the scandals. He had walked into many a church building and found it an empty experience.

Rafael had heard enough about Jesus to get by, but not enough about Jesus to follow Him ... until his life came perilously close to an end. A bit later, I'll tell you how God turned his life around. What amazes me today is not just the brand-new life of my brother, but God's plan to use people like me to connect with people like Rafael – people running from, and wrestling with, belief.

For those of you who already understand what it means to follow Jesus, I trust that this book will enable you to share your faith with confidence. Explaining what a relationship with Jesus Christ looks like doesn't have to be complicated and confusing. A fresh analogy often helps break apart long-held misconceptions.

Jeff's Story

Speaking at a music festival in South Dakota, I bumped into Jeff, who was touring with one of the bands. I talked to Jeff about the concept of this book and he told me to write it fast! Jeff and I had met a year prior as we traveled thousands of miles across the United States by bus. I was speaking on a music tour called *Festival con Dios*, traveling with thirteen bands from city to city. We spent many an afternoon taking long walks and talking about how to live out our faith. He had only recently taken his faith in Jesus seriously and wanted to grow in his walk with God.

Since I had seen him last, Jeff had met and started dating someone. His new girlfriend had been to church before, but didn't have a clear understanding of what a relationship with Jesus really meant. The more they talked, the more Jeff realized that they weren't on the same page when it came to faith and Jesus.

Even though Jeff has been following Jesus for years, he struggles to find the right words to describe his faith. And Jeff's not alone. I speak with thousands of Christians every year, and the more I listen, the more I discover how many have a tough time putting their heartfelt beliefs into words. "She's heard about Jesus. She's been to church, but still doesn't get it. I want her to know Jesus like I do. What do I do now?" That was the gist of Jeff's dilemma. And it may be yours. It is my desire that what I have to say will give you the encouragement to simply let your journey with Jesus affect those around you. Believe me, I don't have all of the answers (or many, for that matter!); but I have been asked lots of questions. I hope that you'll find this look at the Christian journey useful in communicating with your searching friends.

Without jargon or complicated phrases, *Airborne* is your guide to understanding the journey of following Jesus. It's your guide to change your perspective from wondering about God's value to valuing God's wonder!

That type of passionate, intimate relationship can be yours, if you're willing to pursue it.

I've written this book for those people who want to experience the life-changing power that intimacy with God will bring. Only God can change you. It's my prayer that the words on these pages will entice you to pursue Him.

Our journey with Jesus parallels an airplane ride in various ways. Both require trust, commitment, and a ready and willing attitude. Join me as we head for a new adventure – the ride of your life.

1

Boarding
All Rows

A Personal Invitation

Some days are just different. There are the ordinary wake-up, go-to-school-or-work, hang-out-with-your-friend days. And then there are ones you will never forget, moments in life that become turning points.

There was the day when I realized I'm not a tough guy. I must have been nine years old, and a lanky neighbor was picking on my older brother, Miguel. He had to be a foot taller and much broader than me, but something in my brain told me it didn't matter. "John," I told him, "if you don't leave my brother alone, I'm going to beat you up."

He laughed, which made me burn even more. So I hit him in the stomach, like a fly beating an elephant. Before I could take a breath, I was in the air, back thrown against the wall and now afraid for my life! It was my first airborne experience. John then picked me up by the shirt so that our eyes met, his glazed over with annoyance. He slammed my frail frame against the wall and said, "Don't you ever touch me, kid."

That could have been the end of my story. As fate would have it, he dropped me and I discovered that I could run – fast. I didn't wait for his next piece of advice. By the time I got home, I discovered I'd gleaned a nugget of truth. *Don't hit guys much taller than you.* Reason beats violence, especially when the other guy has twelve inches on you.

Seems like a small discovery, but it's been a lifelong help. That was the last fight (if you can call it that) I've ever had. Diplomacy is now my middle name, and it took a tall bully to help me develop that talent.

Meeting Carmen

I've had my share of good experiences as well. When I was sixteen years old, I was playing drums for a local band. One day in walked a girl with black slacks, green shirt, and soft brown, curly hair. She sat in the front row, to my left, and I couldn't take my eyes off her. I couldn't remember the rest of the song list, but I knew that I wanted to know who she was.

Problem number one, she walked in with a guy. But soon I found out it was just her brother. Okay, I had a chance. By the end of the evening, I knew her name: Carmen. The next night, through a friend of a friend, I worked it out (schemed to be exact) for a group of kids to meet at the movie theater. It just so happened that I would be there and would coincidentally sit next to her. We met, had a good time, and by the time we left the theater, I was convinced that we should be together.

Problem number two, she had a father. A strict father. A father who did not like the concept of his daughter with anyone. You get the point. At first, I had "the interview" with her mother. She confirmed what Carmen had told me that her dad had a strict dating policy. In Dad's opinion, no guy was worthy of her and so dating was not an option! Her mom, however, was kind enough to speak to Ray on my behalf and invite me over to their house to get to know him.

I remember entering the house that cold winter evening, walking into the living area, and sitting on the couch to face a reclining chair that resembled a king's throne. Carmen sat next to me and we waited for the king to appear.

Problem number three, Ray looked like a mafia boss. Dark, thick hair slicked back. Perfectly tan skin. I instantly felt like I was in one of the many mob movies I had seen. Something inside told me I was in trouble.

He sat down in the chair. Like a scene out of those movies, I was now scooting farther away from Carmen. My heart now pounded furiously and I kept wiping my hands on my jeans. There was no casual start. Ray went straight to the point.

"So, you want to get to know my daughter," he said in a deep, gruff voice. I thought to myself, "No ... you can have her; I just want to get out of here alive." But I heard myself say, "Yes, sir."

"Well," Ray quickly added, "I love my daughter and I need you to know one thing. I have a machete in the basement and I'm not afraid to use it." And downstairs we went, to the basement, to have a look at his long knife, used to cut down coconuts from trees (or anyone who made the wrong move with his daughter).

Instead of being scared away, I took his threat as a challenge. Carmen was so beautiful and sweet that

I wasn't going to let an overprotective dad stop me from a great relationship. Little did I know that her dad was a practical joker! He has the tough-guy exterior with a teddy-bear heart.

Curiosity brought me to Ray's house. Stubbornness kept me going back. Could Carmen be "the one" for me? Would our relationship last a week, month, year, or even a lifetime? Was this mere infatuation or the spark of love? Would I make it past her dad's machete?

I didn't know then that that night would change my life. After dating for five years, Carmen and I were married in a quaint church not far from the home where Ray threatened my life.

Carmen and I have been married for seventeen years now. I'm a different person because of her influence. She was neat and organized. I wasn't. But I've changed over time. She's rubbed off on me, in a good way. I know that I've done the same for her. When we first met, for example, Carmen was extremely shy, but after years of world travel with me, she's much more outgoing.

From the pages of the Bible you'll find a similar pattern with people who've encountered Jesus in a personal way. Ordinary people are completely transformed after spending time with Jesus.

Andrew's Story

Andrew, a fisherman by trade, was one of the closest followers of Jesus while He walked the earth. The first chapter of the Gospel of John unfolds the details of their first encounter. Andrew had been a student of John the Baptist. John the Baptist was a messenger (prophet), one of the select people with whom God chose to share advance insight into His plan. John the Baptist traveled the countryside telling people to prepare for the coming of Jesus, who would soon arrive to rescue people from their sin-filled lives. We don't know when or how Andrew met John the Baptist, but he was captivated by the message enough to follow him around.

Andrew and another follower of John the Baptist were there the day Jesus walked into the water where John was baptizing people. John announced to the crowd,

> "Look, the Lamb of God, who takes away the sin of the world! This is the one I meant when I said, 'A man who comes after me has surpassed me because he was before me'" (John 1:29-30).

The next day John the Baptist saw Jesus walking by and said to Andrew and his friend,

> "Look, the Lamb of God!" When the two disciples heard him say this, they followed Jesus. Turning around, Jesus saw them following and asked, "What do you want?" They said, "Rabbi" (which means Teacher), "where are you staying?" "**Come,**" he replied, "**and you will see.**" So they went and saw where he was staying, and spent that day with him. (vv. 36-39, bold letters mine)

Looking at this brief encounter, no one could tell that it would be the starting point for Andrew's new life. But as you keep reading this story, you find that Andrew was in the right frame of mind that day to receive direction from God. Andrew was a spiritual seeker. That's not the case with everyone. Some are happy to dismiss the notion of a God as ancient myth or legend. What made Andrew different?

Out of all of the crowds of thousands that heard John the Baptist's words, Andrew was one who took the words to heart. The crowds were curious about this Jesus whom John referred to. But few took the important step of searching the facts for themselves. Andrew did, by talking to John and listening to his references about the coming of Jesus. When Jesus walked up unannounced, Andrew was right there listening, heart open, ready to hear and know the truth.

Many people say they want to know God for themselves. But what do they do about it? Do they hope God's message will simply come to them? Or do they seek out this God, doing the work to pursue this knowledge they say they want? Let me ask you, have you done your homework? Virtually everyone has some opinion about Jesus Christ. What about yours? Did you get it from your research or have you just inherited someone else's opinion?

Andrew did his homework. He knew the prophecies in the Bible about the One whom God would send to rescue people from self-destruction. So it's no surprise that Andrew left John the Baptist to investigate this Jesus for himself.

Andrew was looking for truth. Truth about God. Truth about God's promise of personal change. When he saw Jesus coming and heard John's confession, "This is the one," that was enough – he got up and followed after Jesus to find out more.

Andrew was in a position to receive truth. He was listening. I spend too much time in airports. One of the basic rules that people seem to forget is that when your flight is about to take off, you have to be at the right gate to hear the announcement and get on board. Sounds simple. Yet every time I go to an airport I hear the call, "Paging Mr. Robert Berkman, Flight 478 is ready to depart. Please go to Gate C5 for immediate departure."

If you're not at the proper gate, you can't get on the right plane. Well, how do you find the right gate? There are screens all over the airport displaying all the information travelers need to know. The airline. The destination city. The flight number. The time of departure. The gate number. But you have to look at the screen, find the information on your flight, and get to the gate on time. If you never look, it's a guarantee that you'll miss your flight.

It's like Andrew's encounter with Jesus. It's as if Andrew was in the airport and read the signs to know which gate to go to. When Jesus arrived, Andrew was ready for the adventure before him.

Some people think you have to know everything about God and His Son, Jesus, *before* becoming a follower. Not true! The pattern you see here with Andrew and with dozens of other accounts recorded in the Bible and history is that you only have to know enough about Jesus to trust Him and believe what He says is true.

Let me illustrate. In order to fly from my home in Oregon to England I don't have to have a degree in aeronautics. When I get on the plane, no one tests my knowledge of flight controls or quizzes me on landing procedures. In order to have the confidence to take that flight, I need only to know enough about flying to put my life in someone else's hands. I need to know enough about the airlines to consider them trustworthy. I need to believe in their track record to put my life in their hands, and believe me, every time you get on a plane that's exactly what you're doing – putting your life in the hands of the pilot and crew. You trust them to get you where you need to go.

That's what happened with Andrew that day. Jesus noticed him following from a distance, turned around, and asked him, "What do you want?"

You can tell a lot about Jesus by what He doesn't say to Andrew. Jesus doesn't start with any comment about Andrew's current life situation or with a criticism of past choices. He doesn't ask, "What are you doing here?" or "Do you realize who you're talking to?" Jesus doesn't whip out a list of requirements before Andrew can speak to Him, nor hand him a list of dos and don'ts. Nothing is said about rules that must be followed or adhered to before He'll speak with Andrew. There's only a simple, open-ended question: "What do you want?"

Imagine yourself in Andrew's shoes. The Son of God, perfect in every way, knowing all things, is asking what *you* want. How would you reply? It's a great question to ask when starting your spiritual journey. After all, people investigate what it means to have a relationship with Jesus Christ for all sorts of reasons. Religious and intellectual curiosity. Feelings of emptiness and loneliness. Family tradition. Peer pressure.

Look at Andrew's response. It exposes the attitude of his heart. "Teacher, where are you staying?" He wanted to find out more about this Jesus by being with Him. Jesus quickly replies, "Come and you will see." Andrew and his friend didn't hesitate to accept the invitation. They had the amazing privilege of spending the rest of the day with Jesus.

I wish we knew more details of this day-long getaway. What did they ask Him? Surely they wanted to confirm that Jesus was the person whom John the Baptist called the Lamb of God, the one who takes away the sin of the world. No one wants to follow a fraud. Collecting evidence had to be on their mind. They were spiritual seekers looking for answers to life's toughest questions – just like you are.

Andrew's encounter is a snapshot of what a relationship with Jesus Christ is supposed to look like. People honestly seeking. Coming to the One who knows it all, asking not just for things, not just for a better life, not just for a way out of a tough situation – asking for *Him*.

Jesus gave Andrew an invitation, "Come, spend the day with me, and you will see where I am staying." Andrew took Jesus up on His offer, and whatever they talked about changed the course of Andrew's life. Within a few hours, Andrew ran home to tell his brother that he had found the Messiah (the Promised One from God). Jesus' invitation began with a simple call – come and see.

This seems to be the pattern Jesus used when calling many of His followers. On another occasion, Jesus says to a bunch of fishermen, "Come, follow me, and I will make you fishers of men."

Continue reading John's Gospel. You'll find that Andrew – and soon after, his brother Peter – were used by Jesus Christ to help revolutionize their generation.

This could be your story too, because Jesus is in the habit of taking ordinary people and transforming them into all God created them to be. But how? Life with God has to start somewhere. It begins by answering God's call. Imagine you're at the airport and your flight is about to begin. You're at the right gate. The gate agent calls aloud, "Now boarding all rows." It's your chance to get on that plane and go somewhere. But you have to respond to the call; you have to take steps toward the gate and board the plane. In the same way, Jesus Christ is calling you to spiritual freedom. Jesus says:

> Are you tired? Worn out? Burned out on religion? Come to me. Get away with me and you'll recover your life. I'll show you how to take a real rest. Walk with me and work with me – watch how I do it. Learn the unforced rhythms of grace. I won't lay anything heavy or ill-fitting on you. Keep company with me and you'll learn to live freely and lightly. (Matt. 11:28-30 MSG)

What an offer! It's not a fifty-fifty deal, where you bring your gifts and God brings His. Life with God is 100 percent His idea and His work.

From the Beginning

Take a look at the first book of the Bible, Genesis – the book of beginnings. Everything in the world began with God's words.

> And God said, "Let there be light," and there was light. (Gen. 1:3).

Light. Dry ground. Day and night. Fish and birds. Giraffes and monkeys – God spoke them into existence. Mountains. Trees. Flowers. God landscaped the earth with His very words. Everything was spoken into existence by God. It was all good. It had God's stamp of approval.

Then God took special attention in creating the first man and woman:

> God created man in his own image,
> in the image of God he created him;
> male and female he created them.

The Lord God formed the man from the dust of the ground and breathed into his nostrils the breath of life, and the man became a living being. (Gen. 1:27; 2:7)

God speaks and the sun shines in its place. At His word, the planets spin in their orbits. Yet God changes His tactics when He creates the human race. God is now taking *action*, not simply speaking, to form and shape Adam's body from the ground and then to breathe life into the man's still frame.

Why didn't God simply speak Adam into being? The writer of Genesis links this unique act of creation with God's image.

In God's own design, we are patterned after Him. We are made to look like Him – not physically, because God does not have a body, but in the invisible aspects of being human. That includes the ability to reason, the desire for relationship, and the appreciation of the difference between right and wrong. Human life is special because God chose to make us in His image. Like God, we are sensitive to questions of right and wrong. We are confronted with our own moral decisions about right and wrong. The difference between God and human beings, of course, is that God always does what is right whereas we often make the wrong decision.

In fact, God never makes a mistake. He made Adam and Eve exactly the way He wanted them to be, and He made you according to His plan. Being created in the image of God brings dignity. No matter what you've done, you are valued and are valuable to God simply because He created you. King David, thinking about how well God knew him, put it in writing this way:

O Lord, you have searched me and you know me. You know when I sit and when I rise; you perceive my thoughts from afar. You discern my going out and my lying down; you are familiar with all my ways. Before a word is on my tongue you know it completely, O Lord. You hem me in – behind and before; you have laid your hand upon me. Such knowledge is too wonderful for me, too lofty for me to attain. Where can I go from your Spirit? Where can I flee from your presence? If I go up to the heavens, you are there; if I make my bed in the depths, you are there. If I rise on the wings of the dawn, if I settle on the far side of the sea, even there your hand will guide me, your right hand will hold me fast. If I say, "Surely the darkness will hide me and the light become night around me," even the darkness will not be dark to you; the night will shine like the day, for darkness is as light to you. For you created my inmost being; you knit me together in my mother's womb. I praise you because I am fearfully and wonderfully made; your works are wonderful, I know that full well. My frame was not hidden from you when I was made in the secret place. When I was woven together in the depths of the earth, your eyes saw my unformed body. All the days ordained for me were written in your book before one of them came to be. How precious to me are your thoughts, O God! How vast is the sum of them! (Ps.139:1-17)

In simple terms, there's no such thing as an accidental human being. Whether you were planned or the result of a one-night stand, or even of rape, nothing escapes God's sight. He knew you before you were conceived and saw you grow in your mother's womb. From beginning to end,

He's working out His plan in and around everything you do. You are not alone. Let's get back to Andrew's encounter with Jesus. Can you now see it in a different light? It's not as if Andrew stumbled upon Jesus. The subtle fact is that Jesus was looking for him. God created Andrew to know Jesus. And Jesus' desire from the beginning was to know Andrew. Jesus came to this planet looking for this ordinary fisherman in Palestine.

It's fair to say that Andrew's story has been replicated many times over. He accepted Jesus' invitation to a new way of living. *Come.* Come and see all that God has in store for you. Come and see a future filled with purpose. Come into a relationship with the Creator of the universe and the One who created you in your mother's womb.

It's the invitation of a lifetime, one that I've seen people answer all around the world.

Diana's Story

I met Diana in a small town in Estonia. Just sixteen years old, she came to the club we had rented for a party. However, she didn't know that we rented the club to invite students to hear about how they could know Jesus Christ personally. Diana was one of the first to show up. When pre-recorded music began before the concert, she didn't waste any time, pushing through the growing crowd to be the first on the dance floor. Watching her, I sensed she had no idea what this party was about.

Three bands played edgy music, and band members shared about their personal encounters with Jesus. The crowd loved it and yelled for more. Diana stood right in front as I got up to speak. I told the crowd of students that God made them, loved them, and would accept them –

faults and all. When I told them how a relationship with God was now possible because of Jesus Christ, Diana was stirred. That night, in a club in a small town in Estonia, Diana followed in the footsteps of Andrew. She placed her trust in Jesus Christ to rescue and transform her. She is a new person today. She says that she used to wonder what kind of life she could have in a small town in Estonia. Diana often asked herself, *How am I going to get out of this place?* But now she knows she's right where God wants her to be, and if His plan changes, He will guide her to where she needs to be.

If you want to experience the same ride, you have to get on board. Right now, there are plenty of tickets available. And if you lay hold of one, you're on your way to the ride of your life.

2

Your Ticket

Why This Deal is So Good

A plane ride to an awesome destination awaits those who hold a ticket. Boarding requires a ticket, proving your payment and right to be on the plane. Our adventure with Jesus Christ also requires a ticket. How do we get one? What does it cost? We must know what is required in order to know God and have a seat on the plane.

February 12, 2003. I'm driving home, checking my office voicemail from my cell phone. Nothing new. At least until message number three. I can't remember what the first two messages were about; after listening to the third, the others didn't seem that important.

It said, "This is the White House hospitality office ...." Pause. Replay. "This is the White House hospitality office. On behalf of President George and Laura Bush, you and your wife, Carmen, are invited to join the President and first lady for breakfast on May 1 at the White House.

Please call the following number to confirm that you will be able to attend."

Rewind. Play again. "This is the White House hospitality office ...."

The White House calling me? The President inviting my wife and me to breakfast? This seemed too good to be true. I had to stop and catch my breath. When I finally realized that this wasn't a prank call, the blood started to pound through my veins.

It didn't take me long to call the White House back. And a few days after calling, the official invitation came in the mail. I don't know about you, but I get lots of junk mail. Advertisements for products I don't need or applications for yet another credit card. Most of them end up in the trash can. If I can tell the mail is junk from the looks of the envelope, I don't even open it. But this one piece of mail was treated with the utmost care. Hey, this was my ticket to meet the President of the United States – an honor I wasn't going to miss. I did what you would probably do. I called my parents, family, and friends, anyone I could remember. Not to brag, of course; it's just that news like this is too good to hold back. It's not every day that you get a call from the White House and a ticket to breakfast with a world leader.

May 1st was fast approaching. Carmen bought a new dress. I bought a new suit, crisp white shirt, and red tie. My goal: a picture with the President to hang on my office wall forever. It would be a memento of an unforgettable moment. We flew into Washington two days early. If bad weather hit, we wanted plenty of time to make our connecting flights. We even stayed at a hotel within walking distance of the White House. You don't want to take chances with traffic. The day began with a light drizzle. Arriving at the proper gate, we gave the security guard our names while he scribbled a few notes. Showing our photo identification, we were one step closer. Layers of security checks followed, but soon enough our escort led us into an elegant room with an equally elegant spread of food. Breakfast with the President. The other guests leisurely made their way in and out of the room. I was captured by the paintings on the walls, the ornate furniture, and the sense of history that came alive with every detail. There were no chairs in the room for a sit-down meal. It was served continental style so guests could take in the environment while nibbling their finger food. Attendants ushered the small group into the room where the official program would take place. With military pomp and circumstance, the Secret Service escorted the President and first lady to their seats, as we all stood to pay respect and gain a better view.

The program included music, prayer for the nation, and a few speeches. And then the President's address. Television cameras captured each word for sound bites to be replayed around the world later in the day.

In the end, the President and his entourage walked away. The attendants escorted our group to a balcony where we watched as three military helicopters flew toward the White House lawn. With precision, as I had seen dozens of times on television, the President slowly walked to the helicopter, turned around to wave goodbye to his guests, and was whisked off toward the airport to connect with Air Force One. His next appointment was already waiting.

No handshake. No personal greeting. No photo.

Don't get me wrong. This was a milestone in our lives.

We'll treasure those few hours forever. It's a story I hope to tell my grandkids someday. This was huge – but generic. It was an honor – but not all that personal.

This puts the invitation that God gives all of us – to know Him and experience His life-changing power – in a new light. This is a greater invitation than for a short event with an international figure. It comes from the God of the universe. The Creator of everything you've ever seen or heard. The Master Planner who knows the activity of every living thing invites you, by *name*, into a lasting relationship with Him. This is more than an invitation to breakfast where you see God at a distance. He spends time with you personally. He allows you to get to know Him.

For many, a relationship with God is as distant as my White House experience. You go to church and seemingly get close to where God is supposed to be, but leave without Him ever taking personal notice of you. The experience is pleasant – you have a few good memories and learn a few moral tips. But there's no lasting change.

In the same way, I can say that I know about President Bush, but I don't know him personally. I've read many articles, listened to the President on TV and radio, and even came within 10 feet of shaking his hand. But that's it. That's as close as our relationship gets. Do I really know him? Do I know what he's like? Can I ask him for guidance? Will he be there when I need him the most? No. But it's not the President's fault. We're just not on those terms.

However, his twin daughters know the President that way. Their relationship is intimate. He's raised them. He knows their quirks and gifts. And if they need anything at any time, they have a direct line to the Oval Office. They can reach him on his cell phone.

The Bible maps out for every seeker a path to similar intimate encounters with God. The apostle Paul, who wrote half the books of the New Testament in the Bible, describes the situation in clear terms:

> As for you, you were dead in your transgressions and sins, in which you used to live when you followed the ways of this world and of the ruler of the kingdom of the air, the spirit who is now at work in those who are disobedient. All of us also lived among them at one time, gratifying the cravings of our sinful nature and following its desires and thoughts. Like the rest, we were by nature objects of wrath. (Eph. 2:1-3)

You mean to tell me that the Bible says I'm dead and doomed? Well ... yes! But don't feel alone – you're not the only one. From the first couple on the planet through everyone alive today, each person has rejected God's plan with disastrous results.

In light of this statement, let's go back to the story of Adam and Eve and look at their relationship with God.

> The Lord God took the man and put him in the Garden of Eden to work it and take care of it. And the Lord God commanded the man, "You are free to eat from any tree in the garden; but you must not eat from the tree of the knowledge of good and evil, for when you eat of it you will surely die."... The man and his wife were both naked, and they felt no shame. (Gen. 2:15-17, 25)

Life as it was meant to be! God created Adam and Eve with the freedom to enjoy everything in the garden. All was perfect. They had food. They had a place to live. Adam and Eve had each other. Most of all, they knew God in a way that seems foreign to most of us.

Notice that they were free – not robots. They were free to choose whatever they wanted to eat in the garden. God simply designated one tree as out of bounds. They could have it all – except one tree. And God was clear about the results of disobedience:

"for when you eat of it you will surely die."

There were hundreds, maybe even thousands, of positive choices. Fruits and vegetables of every variety. To keep things in order, heartfelt obedience was all that was required. The man and woman needed to obey God's clear directions (a universal lesson we're still learning). And for a time, Adam and Eve did trust God's leadership. They avoided the tree, and *"the man and his wife were both naked, and they felt no shame."*

There's something beautiful about innocence. I remember when our son was just a toddler. Two-year-old Jonah was so much fun to watch. I have a better understanding of Genesis now that I'm a father. I understand the need for boundaries. While our little Jonah has freedom, he has freedom within boundaries. For example, he couldn't walk up and down the stairs with confidence yet, so we put up a gate at the bottom of the stairs to keep him on the main floor. If we didn't have the gate, he would climb and inevitably fall and hurt himself. Good parents create boundaries. Some things are just off-limits. There was beauty to Jonah's innocence. He loved bath time; it was his favorite part of the day. Just say the word "bath" and he'd pull his clothes off. He'd run around the house naked all day long if we let him. He had no sense of shame. When he keeps to his boundaries, all is well. He has parents to watch over him, food, warmth ... it's the virtual Garden of Eden plus a few dozen toy trucks and Elmo dolls.

As a parent, though, you get a full appreciation for the other half of Adam and Eve's story.

The Bible continues by telling us that the serpent was more crafty than any of the wild animals the Lord God had made.

> The serpent said to the woman, "Did God really say, 'You must not eat from any tree in the garden'?" The woman said to the serpent, "We may eat fruit from the trees in the garden, but God did say, 'You must not eat fruit from the tree that is in the middle of the garden, and you must not touch it, or you will die.'" "You will not surely die," the serpent said to the woman. "For God knows that when you eat of it your eyes will be opened, and you will be like God, knowing good and evil." (Gen. 3:1-5)

Jonah loved trying to pull down the gate. Or better yet, trying to climb over it! We told him "no" plenty of times. He knew that the stairs were off-limits. But somehow in his mind there's a need to push the envelope. He's a good kid, but too much like Adam and Eve. Jonah's free to choose to trust our leadership and obey our simple instructions. Too often, however, he goes the other way and chooses to make a mad dash for the stairs.

And he's not alone.

Dead and Doomed

The serpent offered an alternative interpretation to God's warning. "You won't really die," the serpent says. *"The fact of the matter is, God's motives are selfish. God knows that you'll be like Him if you eat from the tree and so He's said hands off."*

The temptation to disobey is driven by not understanding God's character. God is good. God is love. It's not that He *does* good or *gives* love. He *is* good and *is* love. He's not holding back His best from us by placing limits. A loving God looks at our best interests and acts on our behalf. That's what we see in this garden setting. God provided everything that Adam and Eve could ever want. All He required in return was that they trust Him. Relationships, at the core, are built on trust. Trust is acted out through obedience.

> When the woman saw that the fruit of the tree was good for food and pleasing to the eye, and also desirable for gaining wisdom, she took some and ate it. She also gave some to her husband, who was with her, and he ate it. (Gen. 3:6)

Adam and Eve believed the lie. No, the fruit wasn't good for food. God said that the fruit would destroy them. Yes, it may have been pleasing to the eye, but trusting God's leadership made much more sense. And eating the fruit seemed desirable for gaining wisdom. Who told them that? God? No way. They listened to the voice of the serpent instead of to God. They made their choice and ate the fruit.

I just wish I could read the mind of a child sometimes. Even when Jonah was two, he had an understanding of right and wrong. We told him to stay away from the stairs, and when he got close to them he'd look back at us with his hand hovering over the handle of the gate.

It sounds a lot like the apostle Paul's summary of human nature in Ephesians 2, doesn't it? We follow the passions and desires of our evil nature, which we were born with. Adam and Eve were upright – until they chose to do their own thing. Their legacy has passed on to Jonah.

And to me too. And to you as well. And it's where we get our sense of shame.

Evil Nature and God's Anger

> Then the eyes of both of them were opened, and they realized they were naked; so they sewed fig leaves together and made coverings for themselves. Then the man and his wife heard the sound of the Lord God as he was walking in the garden in the cool of the day, and they hid from the Lord God among the trees of the garden. (Gen. 3:7-8)

The serpent lied to Adam and Eve. He said that they wouldn't die. He said that their eyes would be opened and that they would be like God. But we don't see them suddenly becoming godlike. Instead we see Adam and Eve covered in fig leaves and hiding.

> But the Lord God called to the man, "Where are you?" He answered, "I heard you in the garden, and I was afraid because I was naked; so I hid." And he said, "Who told you that you were naked? Have you eaten from the tree from which I commanded you not to eat?" The man said, "The woman you put here with me – she gave

37

me some fruit from the tree, and I ate it." Then the Lord
God said to the woman, "What is this you have done?"
The woman said, "The serpent deceived me, and I ate."
(Gen. 3:9-13)

Darkness had flooded their souls. Instead of coming clean
and admitting their failure, they tried to weasel their way
out with excuses. It's the beginning of the blame game.
I can relate to Adam and Eve's experience. I didn't grow
up in a garden – I was raised in New York City. But I can
relate to knowing what is right and blatantly doing the
opposite. I bet you can too.

Disobedience has a price tag. Adam and Eve didn't get
away with it. They were caught with their hands in the
cookie jar and they suffered as a result.

First, God cursed the serpent:

So the LORD God said to the serpent, "Because you have
done this, cursed are you above all the livestock and
all the wild animals! You will crawl on your belly and
you will eat dust all the days of your life. And I will put
enmity between you and the woman, and between your
offspring and hers; he will crush your head, and you will
strike his heel."

Then God spoke to Eve:

"I will greatly increase your pains in childbearing; with
pain you will give birth to children. Your desire will be
for your husband, and he will rule over you."

And finally God spoke to Adam:

"Because you listened to your wife and ate from the
tree about which I commanded you, 'You must not

eat of it,' cursed is the ground because of you; through painful toil you will eat of it all the days of your life. It will produce thorns and thistles for you, and you will eat the plants of the field. By the sweat of your brow you will eat your food until you return to the ground, since from it you were taken; for dust you are and to dust you will return."... So the Lord God banished him from the Garden of Eden to work the ground from which he had been taken. (Gen. 3:14-19, 23)

Pain. Cursing. Death. These are new words in their vocabulary. One act of disobedience and the ripple effect is seen everywhere. The serpent is cursed. The woman will experience pain. The man will work harder than desirable and will often find his work fruitless. The garden is now off-limits. The end of their choice is death.

What a contrast! At first, you see God walking through the garden in the cool of the day spending time with Adam and Eve. Now they are running, hiding, making excuses, and paying the penalty for their choices.

Sound familiar? If you've been searching for God, you know what it's like to run, hide, and make excuses. We are born with a sinful nature. From the first family on, the human race has taken a turn away from God's direction. It's not a pretty picture.

In time, Adam and Eve gave birth to Cain and Abel. The brothers brought offerings to the Lord. Apparently, they were both pursuing a healthy relationship with God. Cain, however, allowed his relationship to be tainted by evil in his heart.

He was angry with his brother Abel and killed him (Gen. 4:8). Adam and Eve ate the forbidden fruit; their son Cain murdered his brother. The human race rapidly plummeted from perfection in the garden to perversion in our souls. Within a few generations, *"The Lord saw how great man's wickedness on the earth had become, and that every inclination of the thoughts of his heart was only evil all the time"* (Gen. 6:5).

The saga continues today. The Bible is brutally honest in its depiction of the human heart:

The acts of the sinful nature are obvious: sexual immorality, impurity and debauchery; idolatry and witchcraft; hatred, discord, jealousy, fits of rage, selfish ambition, dissensions, factions and envy; drunkenness, orgies, and the like. I warn you, as I did before, that those who live like this will not inherit the kingdom of God. (Gal. 5:19-21)

All of us also lived among them at one time, gratifying the cravings of our sinful nature and following its desires and thoughts. Like the rest, we were by nature objects of wrath. (Eph. 2:3)

Guilty is guilty.

The fact is that no one deserves to know a God who by nature is perfect. Our sin-filled hearts keep us from knowing the One who's created us and from enjoying His presence and purpose.

Sound depressing? Yes, but that's only half the story! From the beginning God promised an escape plan. What our sin destroyed, God planned to restore. When Adam and Eve sinned and were exposed, God *"made garments of skin for Adam and his wife and clothed them"* (Gen. 3:21). When God spoke to the serpent, He hinted at what would happen in the future: Eve's offspring would someday "crush" the serpent's head. That's a terminating blow.

The serpent won stage one of the battle. Our sin has separated us from God; apart from God's initiative, we cannot enjoy an intimate relationship with Him. Yet God's love for us has never faltered nor failed. At the perfect time, He would send the One who would crush the serpent and destroy the power of sin.

His name is Jesus Christ. He's our way of escape. Philippians 2:6-11 tells us what Jesus did:

> He had equal status with God but didn't think so much of himself that he had to cling to the advantages of that status no matter what. Not at all. When the time came, he set aside the privileges of deity and took on the status of a slave, became human! Having become human, he stayed human. It was an incredibly humbling process. He didn't claim special privileges. Instead, he lived a selfless, obedient life and then died a selfless, obedient death – and the worst kind of death at that – a crucifixion. Because of that obedience, God lifted him high and honored him far beyond anyone or anything, ever, so that all created beings in heaven and on earth – even those long ago dead and buried – will bow in worship before this Jesus Christ, and call out in praise that he is the Master of all, to the glorious honor of God the Father. (MSG)

Jesus' death and resurrection from the dead destroyed the power of the devil (the serpent) and paved the way for you and me to know God. You see, we couldn't come to God on our own. A perfect God can't have sinners like you and me in His presence. Jesus Christ opened the way between God and us. He died so that we don't have to die spiritually. The grave is not the end of our lives! The Bible says that salvation from sin and eternal life with God in heaven is available to all who trust Him to forgive them.

Have you trusted in Jesus Christ as the Way – God's only provision for the problem of sin? Boarding the plane requires a ticket. And Jesus is our ticket.

In order to get on this plane you need proof that there's a place for you. In the next chapter, we will take a look at who Jesus is and how He is your only ticket to the ride of your life. A new start. An awesome destination. These are waiting when you take hold of your ticket and board the plane. "Okay," you ask, "how do I get the ticket? And what will it cost? If I want to know God, what do I have to do?" That's what everyone wants to know.

Read on, because there are plenty of tickets for all who desire them, and the price has already been paid in full – it won't cost you a thing.

3

Transfer Your Trust

Weight on the Lord

By Friday night enough was enough.

For weeks Rafael had been spiraling out of control, payback for the years of alcohol and drug abuse. There was the bronchial infection he could not shake. Hallucinations from mixing medications. Depression.

"Rafael," the doctor said, "you'd better slow down and clean yourself up. At this rate, you're not going to be here much longer."

It was a wake-up call; time to get serious about God.

My brother had heard about Jesus since he was a little boy. He went to church. Read the Bible. But that's it. In high school, friends and parties were more important than the "religious stuff." Now, 27 years old, his body was plain partied out. Cocaine and alcohol started as an occasional thing, but Rafael soon was getting high three, four, even five times a week. The drugs kept him awake, so he'd pop sleeping pills in search of at least a few hours of sleep before work in the morning. If he lost his job, he'd have no money for drugs. Even the respiratory infection didn't stop the cocaine use. My parents found Rafael on the floor of his bedroom convulsing from an overdose of cocaine and medication. Rafael later told us he could *feel* evil in his room, as if demons – the devil's agents from hell – were touching him.

"God, I need you!" he cried.

"Rafael, you need Jesus," Dad said.

Rafael knew he was a sinner, living in rebellion against God's plan. So on Good Friday, the day Christians remember Jesus' death on the cross, my brother had a complete life change. Kneeling by my parents' bed, he came to grips with his past and called out to God for help. "Jesus, I believe You can save me. Save me."

In the last chapter we looked at how far from God we really are. We are sin-filled from day one, and all of us have missed God's standards by a long shot. If that were the end of the story, it would be really depressing. Look at the rest:

> But God, being rich in mercy, because of the great love with which he loved us, even when we were dead in our trespasses, made us alive together with Christ – by grace you have been saved .... For by grace you have been saved through faith. And this is not your own doing; it is the gift of God, not a result of works, so that no one may boast. (Eph. 2:4-5, 8-9 ESV)

My brother Rafael had been a really nice guy. He wasn't the most evil person in the world – not the best, but far from the worst. That's how most people see themselves. Room for improvement, but basically okay.

When it comes to knowing a perfect God, "okay" just doesn't cut it.

Meet the Judge

I was busted recently for driving without wearing my seat belt. Truth be told, I wear it most of the time. But I was on my cell phone when I got into the car and drove away without even thinking about it.

The officer saw me stopped at a red light and pulled me over. I was a bit shocked; I couldn't figure out why he turned on his lights. "Do you know why I stopped you?" he asked.

"No, not really," I cautiously replied.

"I noticed you weren't wearing your seat belt."

Ouch. I didn't bother to explain how good I usually am about wearing it. He already had my driver's license and was writing the ticket.

What I didn't expect is that for this violation you have to see a judge. I'd never been to court before. Speeding tickets, yes. But this was a new experience.

Standing outside the courtroom, the clerk informed me of my two options. Option 1: Plead guilty and pay the fine. Option 2: Talk to the judge and explain your situation.

I figured, what do I have to lose? I knew that I was already guilty. Maybe the judge would be nice and let me off easy. So I waited for my turn to go in.

"Jose Zayas, please rise." Sounds stupid, but with all of the courtroom scenes I had seen on TV, standing before the judge made me nervous.

The judge got straight to the point. "How do you plead, Mr. Zayas?"

"Guilty, your Honor."

"So you weren't wearing your seat belt?"

"No, your Honor."

"Have you ever thought about what would happen to you in an accident without that seat belt on, young man?" she continued.

"Yes, I have, your Honor. And I'll be honest with you. I do wear it most of the time."

"Here's what I'm going to do. This seems to be your first time before this court. Is that correct?"

"Yes, your Honor."

"Even though you've pleaded guilty, I'm going to drop the charge against you and lower the fine," she said as she scribbled some notes on the paper in front of her.

"So this won't show up on my driver's record?"

"No. But I am requiring that you take a driver's safety course. And, Mr. Zayas, I don't want to see you here again. Are we clear?"

"Yes, your Honor."

And with that the bailiff handed back my ticket with the judge's notes on it. I took it to the clerk and this violation was removed from my record.

I was pardoned. My record was clean.

Special Favor

Guilty. All of us are guilty before God. That's a fact. But I learned a great lesson that day in court. The judge may have the power, even though I'm guilty, to adjust the verdict. If the judge can find a suitable means, the penalty can be taken away and the guilty pardoned.

What a great picture of "grace." Another way to describe it is "special favor." God judges that I'm guilty, but His Son, Jesus, stands at my side and says, "I'll pay the bill in full." That's His special favor.

When Jesus died on the cross, He paid the penalty for all the wrong things – the "trespasses" or "sins" – I had done. In the case of my seat belt violation, the penalty was $110. I had the money to pay that, but the judge, in mercy, lowered the payment.

What's the penalty for sin? You ready for it? Death. Yeah. Death. Be perfect or you die. Great news, huh? *For the wages of sin is death, but the gift of God is eternal life in Christ Jesus our Lord. (Rom. 6:23)* But that's exactly what Jesus did for you so you wouldn't have to. He died. He willingly died to pay the highest price for your rebellion.

So now, God, in His mercy, and out of the abundant love He has for us, can and will pardon any person who trusts Him to do it.

Why would God do that? When God looked on us and saw the evil in our hearts, He acted in love by sending His only Son into a human body to walk the earth, so that on the cross He would pay the penalty for us. Jesus, coming to earth to pay our penalty, is proof that God's anger is not the last word. God longs to be with us. He loves us. He proves it by accepting Jesus' death as payment for my sin penalty.

Spiritual life is a gift that God offers all people who would trust in what Jesus did for them. The proof is in Jesus' claim: On several occasions He said He would die and rise again in three days. He did. Christians call this pivotal event in history the resurrection – God raised Jesus from the dead on the third day after He was killed.

People saw Him. They touched Him. They ate with Him. And when Jesus came walking out of that grave, alive and well, hope filled the earth – hope that we too could be alive with God.

But I have to trust God to do it for me.

My Life Is in God's Hands

Getting back to my courtroom experience, I trusted the judge to remove my penalty. When she said, "I'll pardon you," I took her at her word and walked out of that courtroom guilt-free. It's like getting on that airplane. The moment I walk from the jetway into the plane and take my seat, what am I really doing? I don't often think about it, but when I get on a plane, I'm entrusting my life into other people's hands. By my actions I've said, "I trust you to get me where I need to go." Specifically, I've put my full weight on the pilot. I trust the pilot with my life. To be rescued from our sin-filled lives, that's what we need. When we put our trust in Jesus – our full weight on the fact that Jesus paid for our sins and rose again to rescue us – the Bible says He "makes us alive."

The moment you place your trust in what Jesus did for you, God wakes you up to give you spiritual life – the Bible calls this "eternal life." That's life in a relationship with God, for today, tomorrow, lasting forever.

A relationship with God is not like any human relationship – husband to wife, parent to child, friend to friend – that is subject to some degree of disappointment and broken trust, sometimes tragically. Our life with God is the ultimate relationship. He never disappoints, never fails, never leaves. God accepts you, mess and all. Why? Because He loves you, and in His Son, Jesus, the ticket's been paid for.

That's It?

Don't I need to do something else? No! I repeat: No! There's nothing left to do. God paid for your ticket completely. There's no room to brag about how you made your life right enough to be accepted by God. You are guilty of sin until the moment you trust in Jesus to rescue you, and then God immediately gives you eternal life.

What about prayer? Someone may have told you to pray a prayer. Would prayer save you? Well, on a practical level, it's good to talk to God and tell Him that you're trusting His Son to rescue you. But it isn't the prayer that saves you.

Maybe someone told you to turn your life over to God and walk away from all the things you've done; then God would save you. It's true that God doesn't want you to live a sin-filled life, but how can a dead man – "we were dead in our trespasses" – walk away from anything? When you trust in Jesus, God gives you the power to resist temptation and follow His commands.

First, God saves you. That's a matter of trust.

Next, God directs you. You can and will live differently once you've trusted in Jesus Christ.

It just so happens that I'm writing this chapter on a flight back home. To get on the plane, I handed the attendant my ticket. Someone else paid for it, but it had my name on it. And once the attendant took my ticket, I walked on board and took my seat.

I'm now (as I'm writing this) "in the air."

When you place your trust in Jesus Christ to remove your sin, a whole new chapter of life begins. You "leave the airport," so to speak, and start a new adventure with God.

And, believe me, this is no ordinary adventure.

4

Destination Check

Where Do We Go from Here?

I've heard it hundreds of times.

If you've ever been on a flight, no matter what airline it is or where you're headed, the first 10 minutes are exactly the same. I'm so used to hearing it that I tune out.

The flight attendant does the destination check.

"Hello and welcome to United Airlines Flight 478 to Dallas. Please check your ticket to make sure you're on the right flight." (Believe it or not, I've seen a few people grab their bags and get off. Oops, they were on the wrong plane!) Next are the safety demonstrations. They show you how to use the seat belt (duh!), list the rules (no smoking, no cell phones, remain seated while the seat belt light is illuminated, follow all crew instructions), and give you basic instructions on how to find the emergency exits and use the oxygen masks.

Finally, the captain gets on the speaker system: "Hello, this is Captain Jerry, and I want to welcome you to United Flight 478 from San Francisco to Dallas. We'll be leaving the gate in about ten minutes, and we're looking at a flight time of about three hours and twenty-seven minutes. Weather looks good here in San Francisco for take-off, and the weather in Dallas is sunny, the current temperature is 87 degrees, and there's a slight wind at eight miles per hour from the southeast. We're looking at an on-time arrival into Dallas. So sit back, relax, and enjoy our flight. Once again, thank you for flying with United Airlines."

Dave's Story

Dave Lubben grew up in a good Christian family in a good home in a good part of town. Life was good, but in high school he wanted more. Dropping out at sixteen to travel with a rock band, he made choices that led him away from God. "Sex, drugs, and rock and roll. That's what my life was all about," he says. I've heard similar stories many times. "But sitting in the clubs night after night, getting drunk and partying till three in the morning, I'd always wake up empty." One morning, in yet another city with another hangover, Dave concluded, *There's got to be more to life than this*. He started to read his Bible on the road. Little by little, he became more convinced that this wasn't the life God planned for him. Quitting the band, he returned home to North Dakota. More than that, he came home to a personal relationship with Jesus Christ.

Dave "got on board" with God's gift of eternal life. He trusted Jesus Christ to forgive his rebellion. And now what?

Sit Back, Relax, and Enjoy the Ride

I like the plane analogy because of the obvious imagery. Dave "got on the plane" and accepted God's gift of a new life. No one would expect Dave to now fly the plane. That's what the captain does. Dave's the passenger.

The same can be said for your spiritual journey. You're on the receiving end of things. And when you look at the Bible, you won't believe how incredible God's gift really is.

A New Start

Dave had messed up big time. He had not only left his parents, his girlfriend, and school, but also had walked away from God. But that's all in the past. That's old news.

When you trust in Jesus Christ, you start a whole new life. *"Therefore, if anyone is in Christ, he is a new creation; the old has gone, the new has come! All this is from God, who reconciled us to himself through Christ ... not counting men's sins against them"* (2 Cor. 5:17-19).

God doesn't forget anything. He remembers Dave's rebellion. But now He doesn't require Dave to pay the penalty anymore. Jesus took the blame and paid the price in full.

Some things haven't changed. Dave was and is still a musician. His personality's the same. He looks the same. But Dave is totally different. The old way of living is gone. Now he has a personal relationship with his Creator. Dave lives his life with the influence of Jesus Christ.

Dave still sins. He still messes up – every day. I've seen the ego come out from time to time. He isn't always patient and kind, but God is changing him. Dave is a work – God's work – in progress. He's a different person.

Dave is completely forgiven. It's important that you understand what this change means. God is patient. When you
trust in Jesus Christ, you're no longer afraid of God sending
you away forever. You're a part of His family. You are safe.

So here's what I want you to do, God helping you:
Take your everyday, ordinary life – your sleeping, eating,
going-to-work, and walking-around life – and place it
before God as an offering. Embracing what God does for
you is the best thing you can do for him. Don't become
so well-adjusted to your culture that you fit into it without
even thinking. Instead, fix your attention on God. You'll
be changed from the inside out. Readily recognize what
he wants from you, and quickly respond to it. Unlike the
culture around you, always dragging you down to its level
of immaturity, God brings the best out of you, develops
well-formed maturity in you. (Rom. 12:1-2 MSG)

Confidence
The tragedies of 9/11 will not soon be forgotten. I've
met more people who are afraid to fly because of the
ingrained images of terrorists and crashing planes. That's
not to mention other headlines of plane malfunctions,
pilot errors, and lost lives.

Getting on a plane is a risk. Human beings and man-
made machines fail.

But not Jesus Christ!

God wants you to have confidence that when you
trust Him to rescue you, He will keep His promise. God
always keeps His promises. Let me list a few:

Yet to all who received him, to those who believed in
his name, he gave the right to become children of God
(John 1:12)

For God so loved the world that he gave his one and only Son, that whoever believes in him shall not perish but have eternal life. (John 3:16)

Whoever believes in him is not condemned, but whoever does not believe stands condemned already because he has not believed in the name of God's one and only Son. (John 3:18)

I tell you the truth, whoever hears my word and believes him who sent me has eternal life and will not be condemned; he has crossed over from death to life. (John 5:24)

I give them eternal life, and they shall never perish; no one can snatch them out of my hand. My Father, who has given them to me, is greater than all; no one can snatch them out of my Father's hand. I and the Father are one. (John 10:28-30)

Jesus said to her, "I am the resurrection and the life. He who believes in me will live, even though he dies; and whoever lives and believes in me will never die." (John 11:25-26)

God has given us eternal life, and this life is in his Son. He who has the Son has life; he who does not have the Son of God does not have life. I write these things to you who believe in the name of the Son of God so that you may know that you have eternal life. (1 John 5:11-13)

Total confidence. God wants you to know that when you trust in His Son to rescue you, *He will keep His promise.* You don't have to wonder if God's going to go back on His word.

You don't have to worry that the plane is going to crash. God promises the gift of eternal life. That's life in a relationship with God today, tomorrow, every day ... forever.

When Dave placed his trust in Jesus Christ, he received God's gift. Period.

Love in the Mess-ups

The plane has taken off. Dave's experiencing a new life in flight with God. The past is gone. But not the problems.

Dave reconnected with his girlfriend, Maggie. They had fallen in love the moment they met at a high school hockey game. Dave saw the most beautiful cheerleader ever and introduced himself after the game.

"Hi, I'm Dave," he said with confidence.

"I'm Maggie," she shyly replied.

"You're so beautiful and I know that I'm supposed to go out with you," Dave continued.

So much for easing into it! They dated. Dave left. And when he returned they picked things up where they'd left off. Dave had accepted Jesus' forgiveness, but couldn't keep his hormones in check. Even though he knew that sex before marriage was against God's plan, he couldn't resist the temptation. Just weeks before Maggie was set to leave on a cheerleading trip to Australia, the pregnancy test came up positive. Seniors in high school, Dave and Maggie were soon-to-be parents.

How does God react when His children rebel? Is that the end of a positive relationship? Read these passages from the Bible for God's response:

Therefore, there is now no condemnation for those who are in Christ Jesus. (Rom. 8:1)

What, then, shall we say in response to this? If God is for us, who can be against us? He who did not spare his own Son, but gave him up for us all – how will he not also, along with him, graciously give us all things? Who will bring any charge against those whom God has chosen? It is God who justifies. (Rom. 8:31-33)

If we died with him (Christ),
We will also live with him;
If we endure,
We will also reign with him.
If we disown him,
He will also disown us;
If we are faithless,
He will remain faithful;
For he cannot disown himself. (2 Tim. 2:11-12)

If anybody does sin, we have one who speaks to the Father in our defence – Jesus Christ, the Righteous One. (1 John 2:1)

God knows that we will break His standards – that we will choose our way over His way. So there is forgiveness. Enough forgiveness to cover Dave's disobedient choices. Enough to cover yours.

Nothing can separate you from Jesus' love. Can you lose God's gift – your salvation – when you sin? No.

God saved you. That was a gift. You didn't deserve or earn it. It's not a gift that He takes away.

Cool. So can I do whatever I want ... since God is so good?

No way! While Jesus will forgive you and eternal life is yours, living for yourself comes with disastrous results. Just look at what happened to Dave and Maggie.

5

Letting Go
of the Controls

From Diplomas to Diapers

High-school sweethearts. Now married parents. They got married because it was "the right thing to do." Maggie received her high-school diploma as a pregnant teenager. A few months after graduation her morning alarm was the screams of a newborn.

Love. That's why Dave and Maggie came together. *Arguments.* That's why they drifted apart.

Looking back, they both realize they were too young to really understand the implications of their disobedience.

Sin destroys. While it cannot sever your relationship with God (He just loves you too much!), it can destroy the quality of your journey.

In chapter 3, we looked at Ephesians 2:8-9:

> For by grace you have been saved through faith. And this is not your own doing; it is the gift of God, not a result of works, so that no one may boast. (ESV)

God's grace rescued both Dave and Maggie from eternal, spiritual death. But look at God's intention in verse 10:

> For we are his workmanship, created in Christ Jesus for good works, which God prepared beforehand, that we should walk in them. (ESV)

Was it God's intention for Dave and Maggie to get pregnant out of wedlock? No! God has "good works" prepared for those He rescues. God has mapped out a plan for every one of His children. And His plan doesn't contradict His clear commands in the Bible. This one is pretty clear:

> God wants you to live a pure life. Keep yourselves from sexual promiscuity. Learn to appreciate and give dignity to your body, not abusing it, as is so common among those who know nothing of God. (1 Thess. 4:3-5 MSG)

Six months into their marriage, Maggie had divorce papers written up. She didn't want to put up with Dave's selfish lifestyle. And Dave wanted his freedom back. They didn't get along anymore. It wasn't working. Both of them were done.

Wisely, they went to talk with the pastor of the church they had been attending. The pastor told them, "Statistics show that one in two 'normal' marriages end in divorce. And your marriage is not normal. Having a child before marriage increases the statistical chances of divorce. You've got to understand this. Your marriage has no hope!"

This was not the counsel they were expecting. Dave and Maggie thought they would get some encouragement or a quick-fix plan. Instead, the pastor confirmed their suspicion – the marriage was over.

"But you have to understand one thing, guys. You're both followers of Jesus Christ, and God hates divorce. So you've got to get it into your heads: Divorce is not an option! If you'll come to God and surrender control of your marriage to Him, He will save it."

Right there in the pastor's office, Dave and Maggie prayed, "God, take control of our marriage. We give it to you."

Getting Out of the Cockpit

There's a cheesy bumper sticker that I used to see on cars: "God is my co-pilot." Now, I'm not a big bumper sticker fan, but this one especially made no sense to me. The way I see it, if God's in the car, then why are you in the driver's seat?

Do you actually think you can drive better than God? I know what it's supposed to mean, that God is with me everywhere I go. But it shows how off-base our thinking can become.

God isn't "co" anything. He's the Boss. The Leader. The knows-everything-before-it-happens-and-has-all-the-power-to-change-it kind of God.

This journey that you're on will often lead you to give things up. Frequently, my passions and desires are far from God's design. Now that I've been rescued, it should be my life's goal to follow God His way – not mine.

> *What shall we say, then? Shall we go on sinning*, so that grace may increase? By no means! We died to sin; how can we live in it any longer? (Rom. 6:1-2, emphasis mine)

God broke the hold of sin on our lives. Before trusting in Jesus Christ, we couldn't help but live in rebellion. Now that we've been set free and given a new life, we should make it our greatest desire to live in a way that pleases God.

Unending Gratitude

Why bother? If I know that I'm going to mess up, what's the point of trying?

Let me fast-forward Dave and Maggie's story. They left the pastor's office and decided to let God rule over their marriage. They weren't going to follow their own desires (to never see each other again), but follow God's clear commands (to love and respect each other).

It worked. God started to change their hearts. It wasn't easy, but they talked about their differences instead of fighting. When it was easier to walk away, they stayed close enough to work things out.

God was placed at the center of every major decision.

They "left the cockpit" and gave control of the plane back to God.

Dave and Maggie are still happily married (with four children)! In sweet irony, they renewed their vows on a beach in Australia on their 10th anniversary.

Ten years prior, Maggie couldn't make it to the Australia cheerleaders' competition because of her pregnancy.

She paid the price of her sin with disappointment. But by God's special favor and mercy, they got a second chance.

They are in madly in love – because they allowed God to be the Pilot.

Lay It Down

The title of Dave's first CD, *A Place Called Surrender*, shows the reality of God's work in his life and marriage.

The lyrics to "Lay It Down" say it best:

> Here's my life, I lay it down
> Here's my life, I lay it down, I lay it down
> I surrender it all to you, surrender it all to you,
> surrender it all to you
> I let go and give it to you.

They're simple words that seem so hard to live out. Something within me, within all of us, drives us to take control and do things our way. We trust God to rescue us from death, but foolishly don't trust Him enough to hand over the day-to-day operations of our lives.

> Now if we died with Christ, we believe that we will also live with him. For we know that since Christ was raised from the dead, he cannot die again; death no longer has mastery over him. The death he died, he died to sin once for all; but the life he lives, he lives to God. (Rom. 6:8-10)

Can you predict the future? If you're a follower of Jesus, then in one sense the answer is yes. We will live with Jesus Christ forever! That's His promise. "If we died with Christ ... we will also live with him."

But how do we live until that day? Follow Jesus' example:

> "The life he lives, he lives to God."

Jesus said,

> If you obey my commands, you will remain in my love, just as I have obeyed my Father's commands and remain

> in his love. I have told you this so that my joy may be in you and that your joy may be complete. (John 15:10-11)

> I do nothing on my own but speak just what the Father has taught me. The one who sent me is with me; he has not left me alone, for I always do what pleases him. (John 8:28-29)

Jesus, who came to earth as God in human flesh, always did the right thing. He lived to please His heavenly Father. The Father hadn't left Him alone. *Relationship*.

Why lay down your own desires for God's best? *Relationship*. Dave and Maggie for a time saw themselves as enemies instead of lovers. God stepped in and showed them His love. God's relationship with them individually changed their relationship as a couple. It rekindled the flames of love in their own hearts and in their marriage. They are radically different because of their relationship with Jesus Christ. Our motivation to follow Jesus Christ shouldn't be out of obligation: "Man, now I've got to do this and can't do that!" That's not what this is all about. It's about love and appreciation. When you realize how much God loves you and what He's done to rescue you, it should compel you to want to serve Him.

> But friends, that's exactly who we are: children of God. And that's only the beginning. Who knows how we'll end up! What we know is that when Christ is openly revealed, we'll see him – and in seeing him, become like him. All of us who look forward to his Coming stay ready, with the glistening purity of Jesus' life as a model for our own. (1 John 3:2-3 MSG)

Look at this truth carefully. Right now, at this very moment, we are God's children. We are accepted into His family the moment we trust in Jesus Christ to rescue us. The future? We're not 100 percent sure about all the details, but this much we know: One day we will be with Jesus, and we will be like Him. In His presence, we will be like Jesus. Until then I will continue to mess up. I'm not perfect as Jesus is. So what do I do? Knowing that Jesus controls my eternal future, I will strive to live "with the glistening purity of Jesus' life."

Overnight or Over Time?

I've met more discouraged followers of Jesus than you can imagine. In America especially, we want things *now*. We get mad when the fast-food restaurant isn't fast enough! Even with microwaves and text messaging, things are just too slow for us.

That can be a real downer in your spiritual growth. Patterning your life after Jesus Christ is not an overnight thing! There are ups and downs. There are seasons when it seems that your growth is on fast-forward. And then there are days and weeks of living in slow-mo, or worse – living in reverse.

My brother Rafael had been a follower of Jesus for only a few months when he became frustrated. Having been hooked on drugs and alcohol for years, Rafael felt the painfully strong temptation to return.

He knew that going back to the old lifestyle was wrong. Sitting in a diner in New Jersey, with his head in his hands, Rafael admitted that he had slipped on more than one occasion.

He's not alone. Anyone who has tried following Jesus can relate to Rafael's experience. I know that I can. While driving to and from work, Rafael would cry out to God, asking for help. But nothing seemed to change.

I'm not ashamed to say that even though I'm serving the Lord in the way that I do, I struggle. I'm a guy. All guys struggle with lust-filled thoughts. I can be extremely rude and selfish, and have a mouth that often speaks faster than I can think (it's called foot-in-mouth disease).

Sometimes, when I think about all that I've thought and done, I wonder why God still loves me. Feeling like a failure is part of the path of following Jesus. When I know that I've blown it – again – I remind myself of another of God's fantastic promises:

> If we claim to be without sin, we deceive ourselves and
> the truth is not in us. If we confess our sins, he is faithful
> and just and will forgive us our sins and purify us from
> all unrighteousness. (1 John 1:8-9)

At a men's meeting at church, Rafael listened to a speaker who invited people to take a moment with God – to lay things down and trust that God would do a work in them.

Knowing that it was his moment with God, Rafael walked up to the front of the room to pray. He had a unique experience.

He didn't expect it to happen, but it was as if someone cracked the dam in his heart that was holding in all of the pain and guilt from years of rebellious living.

Rafael cried out to God for mercy and let go. Months prior, Jesus had saved him. But on this day, Rafael allowed Jesus to take the controls and steer Rafael on course to safety and victory. From that moment on, the desire for drugs and alcohol was gone.

That was a decisive moment in Rafael's life. God showed that He still rescues mess-ups and chooses to change those who will surrender their lives to Him.

A note of caution: Sharing experiences like this can often lead to misunderstanding. God works uniquely in each individual.

My experience will never look like yours. For some, addictions take years to erase. For others, like Rafael, the victory is instantaneous.

But Rafael's story should make one thing abundantly clear: God does work in each of our struggles when we lay down our pride and surrender that area to Him. Miracles, like mended marriages and erased addictions, can and do happen.

God is the ultimate pilot. He knows where you are and can get you to where you need to be.

What about you? You don't have to be in a floundering relationship or addictive lifestyle to need God's intervention. Wherever you are, you are in a great place to pause and experience the reality of God's presence. You don't have to "feel" something to know God is working in your life. You may not see immediate results. But God is watching ... and working. If you'll hand over the controls to Him, you'll be amazed at how great a pilot He really is.

Why not make Dave's song your prayer?

Here's my life, I lay it down
Here's my life, I lay it down, I lay it down
I surrender it all to you, surrender it all to you,
surrender it all to you
I let go and give it to you.

What do you need to let go of?

_____
_____
_____
_____
_____
_____
_____
_____
_____
_____

Write your own prayer. Be honest with God! You don't need to say things in a special way. Ask God to help you want to let go.

_____
_____
_____
_____
_____
_____
_____

6

The Flight Plan

Stay Calm

April 5, 1999. The day I almost went to heaven.

I was flying from Boston to Presque Isle, Maine, on a small regional jet. Reading my Bible on the one-hour flight, I had no idea what was about to happen.

The flight attendant came out of the cockpit looking as white as a ghost. I travel enough to know that if the flight attendant looks panicked, that's not a good sign. The captain announced, "Ladies and gentlemen, we are experiencing some difficulties up here in the cabin. We have notified Traffic Control and we are set to make an emergency landing in Portland, Maine. Please stay calm and listen to the flight attendant for further instructions."

Yeah, don't panic. Nice advice from a guy who says we're about to make an emergency landing. If there's a good time to panic, this was surely one of them!

It just so happened that as the captain was speaking, I was reading these words of Jesus:

> Peace I leave with you; my peace I give you. I do not give to you as the world gives. Do not let your hearts be troubled and do not be afraid. (John 14:27)

I almost laughed out loud! Jesus spoke these words to His followers nearly 2,000 years ago, the night before His death, and I stumbled onto them at the right moment. "Do not be afraid." I'd never met the captain before, so his "stay calm" speech wasn't much comfort. But the words of Jesus quieted my soul even as the plane raced to the ground.

The Emergency Exit Row Card

The flight attendant quickly asked me to move to a seat in the emergency exit row. "Please read over this card and follow my instructions!" she said.

I'd seen that card before. There's one in the seat pocket in front of every seat on every plane. It's the "what to do if you're in trouble" card. Written by the people who make and fly airplanes, this card is supposed to be your guide through the worst-case scenarios. I'd glanced at it before. Let me tell you, my eyes were glued to it now.

Thankfully, after taking all of the precautions and getting ready for a crash, we landed safely in Maine and stepped off the plane unharmed. I still have the emergency card from that flight – it's a reminder to be ready next time.

God's Book

One of my clearest childhood memories is watching my mom sit at the kitchen table reading her Bible and writing notes in her journal. While her children played in the backyard, there she sat, day after day, reading the Bible with journal in hand.

Even now, whenever we stop by to visit, Mom is sitting in the corner with an open Bible.

I'm grateful for that example. The more that I've read and studied the Bible, the more valuable it becomes. It's more than a book – it contains a personal message from God for you and me.

I don't want to assume that you believe that the Bible is really true. I do. I believe that every word of it is not only accurate, but also useful for life today. But if you have some doubts or questions, you are not alone.

The Bible's trustworthiness is an important issue, but I want to focus the discussion in this chapter on what the Bible is all about. The apostle Paul wrote,

> All Scripture is breathed out by God and profitable for teaching, for reproof, for correction, and for training in righteousness. (2 Tim. 3:16 ESV)

That's the clearest statement in the Bible about its purpose. The words "breathed out by God" and "profitable" set the tone. The Bible is God's book. He worked through many writers over hundreds of years, revealing His plan as they wrote it down.

> Above all, you must understand that no prophecy of Scripture came about by the prophet's own interpretation. For prophecy never had its origin in the will of man, but men spoke from God as they were carried along by the Holy Spirit. (2 Pet. 1:20-21)

Yes, God used the writing style of each individual. But the content and final delivery were orchestrated by God.

"Profitable." The Bible is not an outdated book. For one thing, God never changes.

> For everything that was written in the past [in the Bible] was written to teach us, so that through endurance and the encouragement of the Scriptures we might have hope. (Rom. 15:4)

The goal of reading the Bible is more than to obtain information; the goal is to deepen your relationship with God. As you discover who He is and how He works, you ought to ask yourself, "How will I live differently?" God didn't expect us to somehow supernaturally figure out who He is. He's been involved with people from day one. Read your Bible and you'll learn how to be a better follower of Jesus yourself.

God knows that we need clear directions for everyday living.

An Overview
Maybe this illustration will help. In an airplane, pilots have instruments that can tell them exactly where the plane is and where it's headed. They have way more information than you do as a passenger sitting in your seat.

On many international flights, there are television screens in the main cabin that show you a world map and point out the course that the plane is taking. On the map you can see where the plane started, where it is right now, and where it's headed.

In a similar way, that's what the Bible does for us. We don't have all of the information. God knows way more than we do ... and it will always stay that way! But He's given us enough information to see where people have gone and where we are right now in our relationship with Him, leading us in the right direction.

Some "big picture" thoughts about the Bible:

It's the story of God. The first words in Genesis are *"In the beginning God ..."* The final words of the Bible, in Revelation, give us a glimpse of life beyond this earth – of heaven and eternity. God's at the beginning; God's at the end.

How do we get to know what God is like? You can see the evidence of His work in people's lives, but the clearest picture of God's actions and character can be found in the pages of the Bible.

It's a story about us. There is plenty of history recorded throughout the Bible, but it's not really a history book. The Bible traces the rise and fall of the human race. It tells us how we were created to know God personally. We rebelled against His plan. And God did everything possible to restore the relationship. As you read the Bible, you will find people just like you.

It's our spiritual nourishment. Without food, we'd eventually die. Our spiritual walk requires "food" to keep us strong. Jesus said, "It is written: 'Man does not live on bread alone, but on every word that comes from the mouth of God'" (Matt. 4:4). God has spoken. When we read, understand, and apply what God has said, we nourish our spiritual lives.

Its focus is Jesus. He is the main player in the drama. The first half sets the stage for the coming of Jesus, and the second half shows us who He is and how He impacts the rest of human history. If you read the whole Bible and don't understand who Jesus is, you've missed the point!

Basic Breakdown

The Bible contains sixty-six books. These books aren't independent or unrelated. They were written by some forty writers over a period of more than 1,500 years, yet are in harmony with one another. The Bible can be split into two sections, the Old Testament (Genesis–Malachi) and the New Testament (Matthew–Revelation). The "old" describes life before the birth of Jesus Christ. The "new" describes life as Jesus enters the earth and does His work. It sheds light on who Jesus is and how to follow Him.

In the Old Testament the stage is set for the coming of the Messiah, God's promised rescuer. The first four books of the New Testament introduce us to Jesus Christ, the name of the Messiah. All four books – Matthew, Mark, Luke, and John – describe the same person in their own unique way. The fifth book, the Book of Acts, describes how the Good News of Jesus spread *"in Jerusalem, and in all Judea and Samaria, and to the ends of the earth"* (Acts 1:8) in the years after Jesus' death and resurrection.

Acts is followed by a series of letters written to individuals and churches (Romans–Jude), dealing with specific issues on how to live a Jesus-centered life. Finally, the Bible closes with Revelation. John, one of Jesus' closest followers, was given insight into how world history will climax. There are graphic descriptions of heaven and glimpses of end-times events.

It's So Big ... Where Do I Start?

The best place to start reading the Bible is in the New Testament. Because the Bible ultimately revolves around

Jesus, getting a grip on who He is will help you make sense of the rest of the Bible.

If you've never read the Bible, I recommend that you focus your attention on the Gospel of John. It was written specifically to help you believe:

> "Jesus did many other miraculous signs in the presence of his disciples, which are not recorded in this book. But these are written that you may believe that Jesus is the Christ, the Son of God, and that by believing you may have life in his name" (John 20:30-31).

After reading through John a few times, read the other Gospels – Matthew, Mark, and Luke – for a greater understanding of who Jesus is. From there I recommend that you read the rest of the New Testament, starting with Acts and ending with Revelation. While the books aren't arranged in chronological order, reading the entire New Testament will broaden your horizons on how to follow Jesus day by day.

How do I understand it?

Reading the Bible isn't like reading a novel. Remember, the Bible is God's instructions for us. Because the Bible was written thousands of years ago, originally to people with a culture and customs different from our own, we need to read it carefully to find its full meaning.

Followers of Jesus are encouraged to *do your best to present yourself to God as one approved, a workman who does not need to be ashamed and who correctly handles the word of truth* (2 Tim. 2:15).

It might sound like I'm trying to scare you away from reading the Bible, implying that you're going to mess up what it says. Not at all! I'm trying to encourage you to read the Bible over and over, because the more you read and study the Bible, the clearer its meaning becomes.

Here are some tips on making the most of your Bible reading:

Read it slowly. There's nothing especially spiritual about reading a lot at once. The goal is to understand and apply what God says, not to speed-read.

Ask questions. I don't understand everything in the Bible. Neither will you. When you come to something that seems confusing, write down your question. There are Bible study books that can help you out, or you can ask your pastor or a Bible teacher at church.

Study well. The goal is to apply what you've learned to daily life. But that's the last step in Bible reading. Whenever you read the Bible, ask yourself these four key questions:

What does the passage say? A good translation of the Bible will help. You may want to read what comes before and after a certain verse or passage to make sure that you understand what the writer was actually trying to communicate. For example, John 11:35 says, "Jesus wept." So does that mean that Jesus was an overly emotional guy and that tears are the sign of a good Christian? Of course not. Read the context in John 11:1-34. You'll see that Jesus' friend Lazarus had died. Jesus was touched by the death of his friend.

What did the passage mean to the original readers? This may take a little homework. Knowing a bit about the language, culture, or customs of their day will help you get a better grasp on how the first hearers would have understood it. I recommend using a study Bible. The notes from respected Bible teachers will help.

What does the passage mean for today? If Jesus was talking about farming, is there a principle for your life as a student? The Bible is more than a book of history; the stories of triumph and defeat, obedience and failure are for your instruction and application.

How will I live differently? What have you learned about God that applies to your relationship with Him? This is the "so what" factor. It's a great thing to know what the Bible says and means. Remember, though, that the goal is personal transformation by knowing and loving God. God shows us who He is and how He works so that our relationship with Him will be even closer.

God has written down His plan so that you and I can follow it. But that's not all. God sent a personal guide to help you live out what you believe, the promised Holy Spirit.

7

Enough Fuel to Reach Your Destination

Check the Fuel Gauge

Just a few months into his relationship with Jesus Christ, Rafael needed spiritual power. He couldn't resist the temptation on his own. And God provided.

How? By keeping His promise. Jesus said to His followers:

> If you love me, you will obey what I command. And I will ask the Father, and he will give you another Counselor to be with you forever – the Spirit of truth. The world cannot accept him, because it neither sees him nor knows him. But you know him, for he lives with you and will be in you. (John 14:15-17)

Following Jesus is impossible ... on our own. I'm so glad that Rafael had that "I can't do it" experience so early in his Christian life. God has given us His very words, the Bible, to provide clear direction for everyday living.

But a manual alone will only set us up for failure. The more we learn of God's plan, the more we'll realize that we can't stick to it. Trying to please God in our own strength will work for a while, until burnout sets in.

Burnout. I've been there. In my early teens I knew God wanted me to serve Him by telling others the good news about Jesus. After finishing my Bible training as a young adult, I joined a great organization that works with churches to share Jesus in cities throughout America and the world. The Luis Palau Association moved my wife and me to East Texas to help organize a series of outreaches. It was great. Hard work, but great.

This was a dream come true, working with a godly, experienced leader like Luis Palau. I was just out of college, married, doing what I'd dreamed about. What more could you ask for? The next year we moved to Chicago to join a team planning a huge outreach campaign across America's third-largest city. There were some seventy-five events in sixty days. We arrived six months before the events were going to take place. I never worked so hard in my life! My wife and I worked six or seven days a week, sometimes ten to twelve hours a day.

The only vacation I can remember was a brief trip to visit Carmen's parents in Puerto Rico. And I had to cut the trip short to get back to Chicago for meetings. My time alone with God suffered. I didn't pray much that year. I was just trying to keep my head above water. My Bible reading dropped. There was always another deadline to meet. We couldn't join a local church because I was speaking somewhere every Sunday. We felt all alone, even in the middle of a crowd.

Here's the weird part. I had prayed for years that God would open a door to reach people with His good news. I prayed that God would use me. Now I was being used ... and hated it. I could tell that I was getting cynical. Yet God was blessing in so many ways. Outwardly, things looked good. But inside, my soul was drying up like a prune.

There were some good days, when I went home thinking this is what I wanted to do for the rest of my life. But most nights I slipped into bed hoping that God would get me out of this mess. I just didn't have the strength to do this anymore. I had run out of fuel.

Thousands of people came to faith in Jesus Christ during the Chicago campaign. When it was over, I remember sitting with Carmen in our little apartment in Chicago, feeling completely burned out. Don't get me wrong, I wasn't giving up on the faith. I simply didn't want to serve God this way. Mind you, I had been dreaming about this kind of opportunity since I was a teenager. But now, reality hit. I just didn't have what it takes. Whether it's a temptation we face or some specific thing we're trying to accomplish for God, burnout is a real danger. That's why Jesus prepared for it.

With You and in You

Jesus was about to die on the cross to pay the penalty for our sins when He gathered His closest followers. He wanted to prepare these men for the years ahead. God would soon use them to spread His message. And so Jesus said,

> If you love me, you will obey what I command. (John 14:15)

Salvation and spiritual freedom are a gift. We don't earn our relationship with God. But the sign of a true follower is manifested by heartfelt obedience.

Jesus said the Father would send someone to be with us, described as the Spirit of truth. The Holy Spirit isn't a force.

He's a person. He's God. God the Father sent God the Son to pay for our sin-debt. Jesus rose again and went to be with the Father in heaven. The Father has now given us His Spirit to empower us to live the life that He intended.

What a gift! God knew that the only way we would be able to know His will is for Him to reveal it. And so we have the Holy Spirit and the Bible. As I read the Bible and listen for the promptings of the Holy Spirit, I can figure out what God wants from me and how He wants me to live.

But God didn't stop there. He promised to be with us and in us.

Nothing But the Truth

If there's one person you can't lie to, it's God. Try it. It doesn't work. He knows everything. He knows every part of you. You can run ... but you can't hide.

That fact about God – He is the God of truth – is at odds with our culture that rejects objective standards of truth, that believes truth is subjective, that says truth depends on the situation. "That may be true for you, but it's not true for me."

The result: anything goes.

I understand why that's an attractive concept. It makes every individual the center of what's right and wrong. You can do what you want and don't have to answer to anyone. After all, "it's true for me."

Fortunately, truth is more than a philosophical concept. The Bible teaches that truth is wrapped up in one person, Jesus Christ. Jesus said of Himself,

I am the way and the truth and the life. No one comes to the Father except through me. (John 14:6)

Jesus is always right. As a result, you can trust His leadership. And because of the Holy Spirit, you can know truth (Jesus) for yourself. Jesus said,

All this I have spoken while still with you. But the Counselor, the Holy Spirit, whom the Father will send in my name, will teach you all things and will remind you of everything I have said to you. (John 14:25-26)

I've never seen Jesus. But I've experienced God's presence in a real way because God lives in me (and all who follow Jesus) through God the Holy Spirit. Sounds mysterious, but it's beautiful. I can know God's plan for my life. Why? Because Jesus removed my sin-debt and has given me His Holy Spirit to lead and guide me in all areas of truth.

Power to Trust
Well, how do you receive the Holy Spirit? You receive the Holy Spirit the moment that you trust in Jesus Christ to rescue and lead you.

And you also were included in Christ when you heard the word of truth, the gospel of your salvation. Having believed, you were marked in him with a seal, the promised Holy Spirit, who is a deposit guaranteeing our inheritance until the redemption of those who are God's possession – to the praise of his glory. (Eph. 1:13-14)

When you heard the good news and believed, God accepted you into His family and promised you life that will last forever. The Holy Spirit "seals" the deal. He's like a deposit, a down payment. Someday you will be with God in eternity. Then, and only then, will you get the full benefit of life forever with God. Yet because you received the Holy Spirit when you believed, you have God at work both in and around you *now*. Remember, your salvation is God's idea, from beginning to end. As a matter of fact, you cannot start a relationship with Jesus until God, by His Holy Spirit, leads you. Jesus said,

> No one can come to me unless the Father who sent me draws him. (John 6:44)

While we're still on the earth, God has not left us alone. His Spirit comes to live in us, helping us to understand His plan, comforting us when we're down, and convicting us when we're going in the wrong direction.

> But I tell you the truth: It is for your good that I am going away. Unless I go away, the Counselor [Holy Spirit] will not come to you; but if I go, I will send him to you. When he comes, he will convict the world of guilt in regard to sin and righteousness and judgment: in regard to sin, because men do not believe in me; in regard to righteousness, because I am going to the Father, where you can see me no longer; and in regard to judgment, because the prince of this world now stands condemned. (John 16:7-11)

The Holy Spirit tells us that we are sinners. He gives us a picture of how perfect God is and helps us to see that Jesus measured up to the Father's standard perfectly. Jesus never sinned. When Jesus died, His perfect sacrifice paid the penalty for our sins. He rose again on the third day, ascended into heaven, and was accepted by God. Jesus is the standard of God's perfection. To be with God, we must be as perfect as Jesus.

Great. Not like that's ever going to happen.

Hold on. It's not as hopeless as it sounds.

Through TV Waves

Watching a television program in his living room, a little seven-year-old (yours truly) realized he needed God's forgiveness. Pat Robertson, host of a TV show called The 700 Club, was explaining the Good News of Jesus.

I had never met Pat Robertson, but as I watched him on television with my mom and older brother, the Holy Spirit convinced me of my sin, my need to receive God's forgiveness in Jesus, and the reality that in Jesus I could be set free. At the end of the show, a phone number flashed on the screen. My mom dialed the number, I talked with a counselor, and my life was changed forever.

The Holy Spirit put the desire to receive Christ into my heart. The Holy Spirit sealed the deal. He's been with me from that moment until today. The Holy Spirit will be with me until I stand before God in eternity.

What a promise!

Real Guidance

We won't always get it right. Sometimes we'll follow our own thoughts instead of the Holy Spirit's leading. That's a fact. Yet, the Holy Spirit won't give up! He will convict you and nudge your conscience when you've messed up.

I thank God for giving me His Holy Spirit. Many times His leading has changed my life.

In college the week before finals, I was sitting in a little chapel, praying (believe me, I needed the Lord's help).

I was anxious to get home. I had been dating Carmen for four years, the last two and a half by long distance. We talked on the phone just about every day, but I couldn't wait to see her.

Sitting there praying, out of nowhere I had the nudging that I should take a semester off to get married one year early. Help! I thought my hormones were kicking into high gear. Drop out and get married? That's the craziest idea ... Tempting. After four years of dating my love, I couldn't wait to get married. We had already talked about getting married in the summer of 1994 after I graduated. Why push it up?

Well, I tried to put the idea out of my head, but I just couldn't shake it. I talked to our campus pastor and he prayed with me. "Why don't you talk to your parents and a few trusted friends? Maybe God is trying to tell you something. If He is, He'll confirm what He's saying through other people." I talked to my dad, who's also a pastor. I talked to a few trusted friends. All roads pointed to the same thing. Why don't you just trust God's leading and take the spring semester off? If God continues to lead you in that direction, get married a year earlier. If not, get married after you graduate.

I took three days at a friend's house to spend some quiet time with God. I just needed to know that I wasn't doing this on my own. After day two my heart brimmed with confidence that God was really leading me. It was the Holy Spirit, revealing to my heart His desires.

Things started to fall into place from the moment I left school. I needed a job – got it quickly. We didn't have a dime for the wedding – the Lord stirred family members to pitch in and help without our having to ask.

Carmen's mom came into thousands of unexpected dollars at her job. She paid for the reception. By our wedding day, we had all we needed for the wedding, a car paid for in cash, and plans to move to Tulsa so I could finish college.

We obeyed the Holy Spirit's leading, even when it didn't make sense. Well, Carmen and I were in church a few months later when I saw a brochure on a citywide outreach with Luis Palau.

The brochure called for volunteers and gave a phone number. I immediately turned to Carmen and said, "I need to call that number. I've been looking for opportunities to serve in outreach, and this may be one of them."

I called the number and spoke with Denny Brubaker the following morning. By Monday afternoon, one day after getting the brochure, I was in the Luis Palau outreach office as a volunteer. That summer, I worked as a full-time volunteer.

By the time of the outreach in October, I was hired on the Luis Palau ministry staff.

Here's the point – I had never spent a summer near my college. I always went home to New York to be with Carmen. Yet, because I obeyed the Holy Spirit's leading and got married a year early, we spent the summer of 1994 serving on the Luis Palau outreach.

I was at the right place at the right time to do the right thing ... all because of the Holy Spirit!

But when he, the Spirit of truth, comes, he will guide you into all truth. He will not speak on his own; he will speak only what he hears, and he will tell you what is yet to come. (John 16:13)

How will the Holy Spirit lead you? I've shared just one of many seasons in my life when His leadership and guidance have been mind-blowing. Your experience will be unique, but it's the same Holy Spirit who does the guiding.

An Inside Job

I hope that you're stirred to seek the Holy Spirit's guidance for your life. The New Testament is filled with the real stories of people transformed and powerfully used by the Holy Spirit. The Bible shows us two ways that the Holy Spirit does His work in and through us. The first, and most important, is that He changes our character. When we first trust in Jesus, our lives are still dominated by a selfish agenda. We do what we want to do. Time spent following Jesus changes that. Watching Rafael over his first year of following Jesus has been a kick. Rafael was always a nice guy. He was always fun to be around. Yet, even though I grew up with him, no one really knew what was going on inside.

You knew Rafael from a distance. What was he really thinking and feeling? Nobody knew. That's why he could mask years of alcohol and drug abuse. We were used to Rafael keeping to himself.

Within months of trusting Jesus, Rafael noticeably began to open up. "Jose, for years I really couldn't say anything," he told me. "I was doing my own thing. The rest of you guys were following Jesus. I was ashamed to say what I was doing. And over time, as I got worse, the more I wanted to talk about things. But the guilt and shame ... I just couldn't open up." God set Rafael free. Now he's an open book. If anything, he talks too much!

It can seem subtle, but the Holy Spirit works on our character. He takes the things that don't please God and chips away at them. It's an inside job.

> For the sinful nature desires what is contrary to the Spirit, and the Spirit what is contrary to the sinful nature. They are in conflict with each other, so that you do not do what you want. But if you are led by the Spirit, you are not under law. (Gal. 5:17-18)

There's a real battle going on. Even though you are filled with the Holy Spirit, the "old you" will want to pop up its ugly head – again and again.

God gives us His Spirit, but we do have a sinful nature. You're still human! The goal is to be "led by the Spirit." When the Holy Spirit reveals some part of your life that doesn't please God and He makes it clear how you should change, follow His leading.

The Bible contains God's law. But the follower of Jesus is called to live not under a list of dos and don'ts. Our motivation should be to live a life that pleases God, not just to follow the rules.

> The acts of the sinful nature are obvious: sexual immorality, impurity and debauchery; idolatry and witchcraft; hatred, discord, jealousy, fits of rage, selfish ambition, dissensions, factions and envy; drunkenness, orgies, and the like. I warn you, as I did before, that those who live like this will not inherit the kingdom of God. (Gal. 5:19-21)

What a list! I promise that you'll find at least one thing in there that you can relate to as a problem. I'll tell you mine – jealousy, selfish ambition, and envy. I have a problem with more than these, but I'm ashamed to say that I compare myself to other Christians and get mad when someone else seems to "get ahead."

It's a part of that whole competitive thing. It's stupid. It's immature. But left unchecked, I'm going to slip into finding out what's best for *me* and manipulate the situation to my benefit.

My own brothers laugh at me. "There goes the manipulator again." Ouch. Sometimes I don't even know that I'm doing it.

Carmen will have to tell me, "Do you realize what you just did?"

"No, I didn't."

The Bible gives us a strong warning as well as great hope. We need both. The warning is that *"those who live like this will not inherit the kingdom of God."* That doesn't mean that true Christians will lose their salvation.

It does, however, remind us that not everyone will be saved. Not everyone in churches or Christian fellowships will enter heaven. There are those whose lives show they are still ruled by sin. They are fooling themselves if they think they will get to heaven.

Sometimes too, genuine Christians may allow specific sins to take hold of their lives. This carries ugly consequences. Their path to heaven will be more complex and more painful. You'll miss out on many of the good things God would have given you in this world. Besides, there are rewards for honoring God. These rewards are not passports into heaven, but life is much more enjoyable when you do things His way!

I've seen followers of Jesus live for a time in disobedience to God's clear commands. It's not worth it. You always lose when you sin.

Do not be deceived: God cannot be mocked. A man reaps what he sows. The one who sows to please his sinful nature, from that nature will reap destruction; the one who sows to please the Spirit, from the Spirit will reap eternal life. (Gal. 6:7-8)

You can't fool God. Live for yourself and you will pay for it. God does discipline His children. You don't want God spanking you – it hurts!

The flip side is the hope that God gives.

But the fruit of the Spirit is love, joy, peace, patience, kindness, goodness, faithfulness, gentleness and self-control. Against such things there is no law. Those who belong to Christ Jesus have crucified the sinful nature with its passions and desires. (Gal. 5:22-24)

God will change you. When you receive the Holy Spirit, He begins to work on your character, the real you, so that who you are begins to look more and more like Jesus – loving and patient and kind, etc. I'm not nearly as self-centered as I used to be. Still working on it, but the Holy Spirit has given me the self-control to put other people before my desires.

The Holy Spirit wants to change you, but you do have a major part to play. We are called to "crucify" or kill the sinful nature. You're given choices every day. For example, when lust kicks in, you can choose to turn away from the images causing it, or when you are blamed for a mess you didn't create you help clean it up anyway. It's tough at first. But it can become a second nature over time with the help of the Holy Spirit.

When someone does something against you, your natural reaction is to get back at that person – and harder than he/she hit you! It takes a choice to trust God's leadership and demonstrate love.

The more you choose to follow God's way, the deeper and broader the Holy Spirit will produce "fruit" in you that pleases Him.

Again, I'm not suggesting that you'll always get it right. But as you look back, the pattern in the next few years should be a more God-centered life than a selfish one.

I wish you could spend a day with Rafael. He's not perfect. But since trusting Jesus Christ, he's headed in the right direction. The same can be said of you.

8

One Plane, Many Passengers

Growing in Groups

"Please don't leave me in Kenya. Whatever happens, get me on this plane to London, get me a doctor, and don't leave me." With that I bent over and threw up again.

I've traveled the world with Dave Lubben and Jeramy Burchett. Dave plays the guitar and sings; Jeramy plays drums. We've laughed together. Cried together. And, on more than one occasion, almost died together.

This time I thought I was the one headed for eternity. We had just finished a mission trip to Uganda in eastern Africa. There we were, crazy guys sharing Christ to crowds of thousands ... in the middle of a civil war! We survived – no doubt it helped to have guards armed with machine guns. In spite of the guns and war, many young people placed their trust in Jesus.

The night before we were to return home, I started feeling sick. I didn't get any sleep that night. By the time the sun rose I was miserable: full-blown fever, sweats, achy bones, and upset stomach.

I survived the short flight from Uganda to Kenya. Now two long flights lay ahead: Kenya to London, London to America. Sitting in the Nairobi airport, I started to lose my bearings. I couldn't walk or think straight. Tottering toward our gate, I almost passed out.

At times like this you need to know that you're not alone. Dave and Jeramy stepped in. They talked to the flight attendants and got my seat changed so I could stretch out. They stayed with me all the way through. Without them I would have been in a real mess.

Back in the United States, I was still sick for a week. The doctors figured that I caught a virus that needed to work its way through my system. I thank God for the doctors' help and medication. But I'm more grateful for friends who got me home safely.

Never Travel Alone

What does this have to do with your spiritual journey?

Everything.

You weren't made to travel alone. God designed you to connect with other travelers, to grow in groups.

Look at Jesus. He's God in human flesh, yet even He didn't travel alone. Wherever you find Jesus, you usually see a group.

Twelve men made up Jesus' closest crew. Some were fishermen, others were tax collectors and political activists. Thousands followed Jesus around as He taught and did miracles. They had one thing in common: Jesus.

As He approached the hour when He would leave this world and return to His Father in heaven, Jesus invited

His closest group of friends to a special meal and to hear last-minute instructions. Everything He said and did that night was carefully planned and extremely important to the success of His mission. Jesus told them,

> Remain in me, and I will remain in you. No branch can bear fruit by itself; it must remain in the vine. Neither can you bear fruit unless you remain in me. (John 15:4)

And He's right, of course. Without Jesus we're powerless to live a life that pleases God. Without a fresh and ongoing relationship with Jesus, we'll dry up. We won't be productive.

He continued,

> As the Father has loved me, so have I loved you. Now remain in my love. If you obey my commands, you will remain in my love, just as I have obeyed my Father's commands and remain in his love. (John 15:9-10)

How do we stay connected and remain in His love? Find out what God wants you to do and obey Him. Sure, we'll mess up. We'll never be perfect this side of eternity. But Jesus wants you to know that as you sincerely desire to do what He wants, you can count on experiencing God's love every step of the way.

So far this is personal. You and God. God and you. But if you stop there you'll miss the secret to how your relationship with Jesus will grow.

> This is my command: Love one another the way I loved you. This is the very best way to love. Put your life on the line for your friends. You are my friends when you do the things I command you. I'm no longer calling you

servants because servants don't understand what their master is thinking and planning. No, I've named you friends because I've let you in on everything I've heard from the Father.

You didn't choose me, remember; I chose you, and put you in the world to bear fruit, fruit that won't spoil. As fruit bearers, whatever you ask the Father in relation to me, he gives you.

But remember the root command: Love one another. (John 15:12-17 MSG)

God loves His Son Jesus. Jesus loves His friends – that's you and me if we obey Him. And Jesus tells us exactly how to stay in that love relationship. Lay down your life for your friends. This wasn't just some hypothetical phrase that Jesus hoped would fit on a plaque on a wall. It's how the Christian faith is to be lived out. Friends sacrificing for friends. Jesus chose you because He loves you, and He calls you to obey Him. You'll find your greatest satisfaction walking out your journey of faith with other friends – *with other followers of Jesus*.

Your friends will make or break you. I'm not suggesting that you never hang out with people who aren't Christians. I'm not saying you should stay away from non-Christians, that you avoid friends who do not follow Jesus. No, you want to be an influence for Jesus Christ in their lives, and that's difficult if not impossible to do from a distance.

But you want the influencers in your life to be followers of Jesus. Here's what I've done: I've found people like Luis Palau, who is older than me, wiser than me, and who's followed Jesus longer than me. He's not the guy I hang out with every Friday night, but he's a friend. You could call him a mentor. All of us need someone who knows us, cares about us, and is willing to challenge us when he/she sees things in our lives that aren't pleasing to God.

The first followers of Jesus who heard His command to love each other – the crew of twelve who were with Jesus the night before He died – didn't always get along. They were competitive and often selfish. Each wanted to be closest to Jesus. They came from different parts of the country, different levels of society, and held different political persuasions. But God called them to a community. You also need other people to help you follow Jesus Christ.

Jesus Brought Us Together

In some ways I'm exactly like my friend Dave; in other ways we're polar opposites. We're both terribly competitive. I insist that every contest be governed by The Zayas Rule: We keep playing until I win at least once.

I have to win.

On the last night of a long trip in Romania, Dave and I played Ping-Pong until the sun rose, all because of The Zayas Rule. He's good. I stink.

Now, when it comes to food we're opposite extremes. Here's Dave's diet: beef and potatoes. He grew up in North Dakota, and I'm not exaggerating when I say the guy lives on beef and potatoes. Or when in a foreign country, it's a hamburger and fries (same thing, different package). He might be the most boring eater I've ever met.

Me, I want the wildest thing on the menu. I'll try anything once, except liver or the flesh of some other organ. It's fun to watch Dave's expressions when I eat something strange. He cringes while I laugh.

Dave and I have been serving Jesus together for more than a decade. He's had a huge influence on my life. He's encouraged me. He's challenged me. He's told me off when I needed it. Sitting in that airport in Nairobi, I was so glad that Dave and Jeramy were there. I needed them then. I need them now. Community. Jesus pours out His love to us through other people. I can go on and on about people who have shaped my thinking and invested in my life. John and Nancy, volunteer leaders for our church youth group, were like a second set of parents during my teen years. During a winter retreat weekend, I was acting like a real pain in the you-know-what. I kept talking while they were leading a group. I kicked the annoying side of my personality into high gear.

Finally, Nancy pulled me into the hall and set me straight. At the time it seemed harsh. "Hey, isn't she here to love and help me?" Now I know that's exactly what I needed.

C-o-m-m-u-n-i-t-y Spells Church

Community is what the church is all about. When I was a kid, I thought "church" was a building you went to on Sunday to do spiritual exercises. As I've studied the Bible, I've learned that "church" has little to do with walls and chairs.

Jesus rarely spoke the word "church." When He did, He clearly wasn't talking about a building:

> On this rock I will build my church, and the gates of hell shall not prevail against it. (Matt. 16:18 ESV)

Jesus was talking about people – the whole company of people who would travel together as His followers, united by their faith in their Leader-Savior, down through the centuries.

Yes, churches own buildings and people do meet there, but the church is a community of people, flaws and all, in love with God, learning to love one another.

Notice I said "learning." There's an old cliché: "If you ever find a perfect church, don't join it. You'll ruin it." No one is perfect. No community of Jesus followers is perfect. That's why Jesus *commanded* His followers to love one another. He knew how hard it would be for us to do!

I hear the same complaint in different forms – often something like: "I love Jesus. It's so-called Christians I can't stand." You may have been burned by the hypocrisy of a Christian or visited a church only to leave more turned off than turned on. I've been a part of many churches. I've seen my share of scandals and disappointments. But when I look at my own life and see all of my shortcomings, I'm reminded that there are no perfect friends, no perfect places, no perfect churches.

You only have to read the Book of Acts, the New Testament book that tells how Jesus started to build His church through the power of the Holy Spirit, to get a snapshot of the first group of Christians. Look at the good days:

They prayed together (Acts 2:1; 4:24).

They shared their money and property (2:44).

They met to eat and worship (2:46).

They discussed their disagreements (6:2).

They met to celebrate what God did through them as they witnessed (14:27).

Sounds like the ideal place to be. But don't forget the flip side. Look at the tough days:

They were made fun of (Acts 2:13).

They were threatened (4:21).

Some lied and cheated (5:1-11).

They were arrested and beaten for their faith (5:18, 40).

Some were killed for their faith (7:59-60; 12:2).

Persecution spread and being a Christian meant danger (8:1-3).

There were major disagreements among their leaders (15:1-21, 36-41).

If that's not convincing enough, consider this: Most of the New Testament letters were written to churches that were dealing with people problems. Some in the church were abusing power. Others taught lies and misrepresented Jesus' message. Many were flat out in rebellion to the truth. It happened nearly 2,000 years ago. It happens today.

Life isn't easy. Following Jesus Christ often comes with great challenges – even persecution. I remember meeting with pastors of "underground," or non-registered, churches in China. It's illegal for these groups to meet for worship. Sharing their faith in public may bring interrogation. Intimidation. Imprisonment. And yet they gather. In apartments. In shop storerooms. Late at night or early in the morning. When it would be much easier to follow Jesus as a single traveler, these believers joyfully risk safety and stand to worship God together. Why? To experience the power of Jesus' love expressed through living with and serving one another.

On the other side of the globe, in Africa, a pastor told me, "It's so dangerous here that I've sent my children away for schooling. I just couldn't leave here though. The people need me. The Good News of Jesus is spreading. God is at work here. And so I stay."

Jesus said that the greatest love is shown when people lay down their lives for their friends.

We're in this together. If you're a follower of Jesus, then you're a part of this great company of friends.

Jesus wants you to live out your life with other followers. So whatever you do, don't give up on God's family, the church. It's not perfect ... yet – but neither are you. The church, however, is the one living organization – really, *organism* is the better word to describe what the Bible calls "the body of Christ" – that Jesus said He would masterfully build and vigorously protect.

> For no one ever hated his own flesh, but nourishes and cherishes it, just as Christ does the church, because we are members of his body. (Eph. 5:29-30 ESV)

> Just as each of us has one body with many members, and these members do not all have the same function, so in Christ we who are many form one body, and each member belongs to all the others. (Rom. 12:4-5)

I'm usually cautious about giving advice. But let me share some personal guidelines that may help you find a group of Christians to "grow with."

Find a church where Jesus is the central focus. Sounds like a paradox, but there are churches that focus more on a program or personality than the person of Jesus.

Make sure that the Bible is taught and believed. You're sure to get distracted in your faith when you value people's ideas and opinions more highly than God's clear teaching. If a church chooses to disregard any part of the Bible as valid and practical for today, watch out!

Look for signs of love and concern. You can teach the truth and still forget that Jesus called us to love and lay down our lives for one another. As you meet people in the church, you ought to find genuine signs of humility and concern. I'm talking about more than a plastic smile as you walk in the door. Spend some time with people who've been there for a while and you'll sense a warm welcome or a distant chill.

Commit to more than a weekend gathering. The point of joining a church is not to make it to the weekend services.

That's a great place to start, but only the beginning. Look for two to five people with whom you can spend more time.

Maybe there's a Bible study or discipleship group that meets in a home. That's where I've grown the most – in an environment where I can be real, ask questions, and build relationships.

There are lots of other practical things I could add, but this should be enough to get you started.

Don't do life alone. Follow Jesus by connecting with a group of fellow travelers.

9

Buckle Up–
Turbulence Ahead

Why This Won't Be an Easy Ride

"Trust in Jesus Christ and your life will be better," said the preacher.

In one sense that statement is true. When your sin is removed and you're in a right relationship with God, hey, that's not a bad thing. It's better than you were before.

But Jesus never promised His followers an easy ride. Quite the opposite.

> In this world you will have trouble. But take heart!
> I have overcome the world. (John 16:33)

Turbulence is a crazy thing. I was flying in a small prop plane in Wyoming. The wind was whipping so fast I was sure the plane was going to fall apart. It was better than any roller-coaster ride – left to right, up and down. The only thing we didn't do was turn upside down – and that's good, because that's a sure sign you're about to crash.

Turbulence is wind. If you look outside the window of the plane, you can't see it. You can't see where it's coming from and how hard it's hitting the plane. You feel it. I've flown so much that it doesn't faze me anymore. Experience is a great teacher. But I have seen people freak out when the plane shakes. They'll grab their seat. Duck their head. I've seen a few burst into tears. What they don't realize is that the pilot is in complete control. You can't see it, but inside the cockpit the pilot is guiding the plane through patches of turbulence to a still, cruising altitude.

In chapter 2 we were reminded of how evil human nature really is. We're tempted to do wrong, while the Holy Spirit is cheering us on to live for God. We have "control" over that kind of turbulence. If you have the Holy Spirit, you can choose to do the right thing. But what about forces beyond your control?

Corporate Downsizing

I grew up in New York City. Dad, Mom, two brothers, a sister, and me (and an occasional pet). My mom stayed home to raise us. Dad didn't make much as an accountant with General Electric. Six mouths to feed on one income made things tight. We never ate out much, didn't drive a fancy car (unless you consider a Volkswagen station wagon fancy). We lived in a small apartment in Brooklyn for the first 10 years of my life. I loved it. Things were cramped, but it was cool. Through a series of what I would call miraculous events, we were able to buy a home in Staten Island.

I grew up looking out of a third-story window with bars on it, peering down to cement, asphalt, and two green bushes. So to look out and see a lawn was like going to heaven. I was so used to noise that it took me weeks to learn how to fall asleep in our quiet new neighborhood. We couldn't have been happier. Life was good. God had blessed us more than we deserved.

That good, happy life was shattered when Dad came home with news that GE was moving their headquarters to Connecticut. Dad was a leader at our church, teaching Bible studies and helping to start new churches across New York City. GE offered a generous package for our family to move. They'd buy the house, give us extra money, and resettle us in Connecticut.

My parents prayed. They were confident that God wanted us to stay and serve Him in New York. And so Dad declined the offer.

I learned a new term called "corporate downsizing." My dad couldn't predict it, but companies were letting people go left and right. Dad sent hundreds of resumes and had countless interviews. "Not hiring right now." "You're overqualified." "We'll hold on to your resume should something come up." After a while, I didn't even want to ask Dad how the interview went.

Now, you need to know something about my father. He's the most responsible person I know. He's no slacker. He lives by the creed, "If you're not going to do it right, don't do it at all." So to see him strike out every time hurt.

Fast-forward two years. That's right, for more than two years my dad couldn't find work at the same pay he was used to. Things got tight. Things got tighter. Things got flat-out desperate.

Why? If you've ever asked God "Why?" you're not alone. I would stay awake and cry out to God, with real tears, asking God to rescue us from this mess. These were my junior-high and high-school years. We barely had money for food, let alone new clothes. I felt like a total reject, and there was nothing I could do about it.

This is where faith shines best. My parents, instead of griping and complaining, leaned on God for help and peace. Things got really bad. But they knew that they had followed God's clear direction in staying with our church in New York.

An eviction notice came. The two years of underemployment turned into four. There were odds-and-ends jobs, but not enough for a family our size. For more than two years, we lived in a house that had been officially repossessed. At any time, the marshal could come and kick us out onto the street.

> We do not want you to be uninformed, brothers, about the hardships we suffered in the province of Asia. We were under great pressure, far beyond our ability to endure, so that we despaired even of life. Indeed, in our hearts we felt the sentence of death. But this happened that we might not rely on ourselves but on God, who raises the dead. (2 Cor. 1:8-9)

Boy, can I relate to the apostle Paul's lament. My older brother, Miguel, and I had part-time jobs at McDonald's. We would sometimes pass on our meager checks just to help put food on the table. Listening to my dad cry out to God in his room, with door locked and the pressure on, is something I'll never forget. Just writing about it brings tears to my eyes. Those were painful years, and we were following Jesus. Please explain that to me! It's not like we were in rebellion or something. My parents have been more faithful to God than any couple I've ever met. Why did this happen to us? Believe me, when I get to heaven, I'd like to find out.

Turbulence can break you or strengthen your resolve. My parents believed that God had a plan in all of this. Coming through it, I left with faith of my own. God provided every step of the way. Over those four years, the cupboards were never empty. We had clothes on our backs. We even had a car – beat-up, oil leaking, but it got us around. In turbulent times you see what the plane is really made of. We were shaken. God wasn't. He brought us through.

Talk about miracles. One Sunday morning, my dad had 10 cents to his name. That's it, with a family of six. He was sitting in church and the Lord impressed him to give it in the offering. "God, this is all that I've got," he prayed. "But I trust You. It won't do me any good anyway! Here it is, Lord." No one knew it was Dad's last dime, but the Lord led people to come up to him and give him money. Some knew about what we were going through, others did not. Our family left church that day with $400 in cash and groceries. Explain that one to me!

In this world you will have trials and trouble. It's part of the journey. It's God's design to allow things to happen that will draw our attention to His ability to care and provide. Do you trust God? Be careful how you answer that one. I learned during four desert years that God can provide food and water to live.

Trials and turbulence are really for our good. Don't believe me? Please get one thing clear: You are not God. I am not God. So we shouldn't expect to know all of the hows and whys of what God does. There are parts to life that will remain a mystery.

The apostle Paul was traveling to Asia to spread the message of Jesus. What did he experience? Hardships, pressure, despair, the sentence of death.

This happened, Paul wrote, that we might not rely on ourselves but on God, who raises the dead. (2 Cor. 1:9)

Paul felt like he couldn't run the race anymore. He'd been stoned by his opponents and left for dead. Beaten up because he wanted to share the love of Jesus. Go figure.

Yet, he looked at hardship from God's perspective. "God, I trust You. If You can raise Your Son from the dead and give me eternal life, then I will trust You with my day-to-day problems."

I'd like to say that turbulence is a one-time thing. I can't. There have been and will be seasons to life that are scary.

God pulled Paul through. He pulled my family through. And He will see you through to the end.

He has delivered us from such a deadly peril, and he will deliver us. On him we have set our hope that he will continue to deliver us, as you help us by your prayers. Then many will give thanks on our behalf for the gracious favor granted us in answer to the prayers of many. (2 Cor. 1:10-11)

How can turbulence help you? I was flying into Portland, Maine (not the time that we almost crashed), and we were the last plane to land before the airport was closed due to bad weather.

After circling the airport for 40 minutes, the captain announced, "Even with the strong winds, we have been cleared for landing. Make sure that you're buckled in, and check to make sure that all of your belongings are safely stored. This will be a rough landing."

This was a big Boeing 757, no little prop job. "Great," I thought, "here we go again."

As we approached the runway, the plane suddenly turned sideways. I could see the runway, then we were heading way off course. The pilot took a sharp turn back toward the runway and slammed the plane onto the pavement. I mean *slammed*!

When we reached our gate, the pilot stood at the open cockpit to say goodbye as people deplaned. Let me tell you, I guarantee he heard more "Oh, thank yous" than ever.

> We also rejoice in our sufferings, because we know that suffering produces perseverance; perseverance, character; and character, hope. (Rom. 5:3-4)

Tough times cause you to put your hope in God. They wake us up to the fact that without God we'd crash ... and fast.

When Hell Breaks Loose

Many times we cause some of our own trouble by our bad choices which lead us down troubled and dangerous roads.

> When tempted, no one should say, "God is tempting me." For God cannot be tempted by evil, nor does he tempt anyone; but each one is tempted when, by his own evil desire, he is dragged away and enticed. Then, after desire has conceived, it gives birth to sin; and sin, when it is full-grown, gives birth to death. (James 1:13-15)

There are other times when we may not be sure whether we're suffering for our own faults or more generally. We may face job losses and tough times. Sometimes bad things do happen to good people. That's when we have to trust God's leadership in a difficult world.

And as if those aren't tough enough, we have an enemy out to attack us.

> Be self-controlled and alert. Your enemy the devil prowls around like a roaring lion looking for someone to devour. Resist him, standing firm in the faith, because you know that your brothers throughout the world are undergoing the same kind of sufferings. (1 Pet. 5:8-9)

You don't want to mess with the devil. He's been around a lot longer than you and knows what makes you tick. He's had centuries of practice to hone his trade as a liar and murderer (John 8:44). No red outfits and pitchforks. He's evil and on a mission to destroy you.

Why is Satan out to get you? It's a family feud – he hates God and the children of God. When you joined God's family, you were added to the devil's massive hit list. He used to be one of God's highest-ranking angels, but was banished from heaven after starting an uprising. In his own twisted pride, Satan (then called Lucifer) thought he was equal to God. He still believes his own lie.

Now, there's no reason to be afraid of the devil. Look carefully at how Peter described him: *"The devil prowls around like a roaring lion looking for someone to devour."* If you're a child of God, the devil has no ultimate power over you.

110

Jesus Christ, the victorious one, lives in you. The devil can set traps – and he does. He can manipulate people to do things against you – and he does. *"Satan himself masquerades as an angel of light"* (2 Cor. 11:14).

But there remains a bottom line – when Jesus died on the cross and rose again, He defeated the devil and all of his demons. It goes back to the initial battle that started the feud:

> Now the serpent was more crafty than any of the wild animals the LORD God had made. He said to the woman, "Did God really say, 'You must not eat from any tree in the garden'?" (Gen. 3:1)

He's a sneak. He lies, cheats, and steals. He puts a gentle twist on the truth, hoping that we will recognize his version as the truth. God told Adam and Eve not to eat from one tree or they would die. Satan twisted God's words and convinced the woman that God was lying to them:

> You will not surely die.... For God knows that when you eat of it your eyes will be opened, and you will be like God, knowing good and evil. (Gen. 3:4-5)

The man and woman bought the serpent's lie and sinned. So have we.

The devil may succeed because he knows the Bible better than you do. He twists the Bible to make it prove his distorted lies. When he tried this same old trick on Jesus, Jesus shot back with the truth.

> The tempter came to him and said, "If you are the Son of God, tell these stones to become bread." Jesus

answered, "It is written: 'Man does not live on bread alone, but on every word that comes from the mouth of God.'" (Matt. 4:3-4)

The devil says, "Use God's power for your own good." Jesus says, "I don't need to make bread; I'll feed on God's word."

The devil tried a second time:

"If you are the Son of God," he said, "throw yourself down. For it is written: 'He will command his angels concerning you, and they will lift you up in their hands, so that you will not strike your foot against a stone.'" Jesus answered him, "It is also written: 'Do not put the Lord your God to the test.'" (Matt. 4:6-7)

Once again, he's trying to play with Jesus' ego. "Jesus, if You're the Son of God, prove it. After all, God said He'll protect His Son."

Jesus quoted the Bible with power: "We're not to test God." In other words, Jesus said, "I know who I am. I'm not playing with God's power for My benefit."

Here we learn another lesson about the devil's program. He's persistent! He didn't give up after one punch from Jesus, and he's not going to stop attacking you.

On the third try, the devil pulled out all of his tricks:

Again, the devil took him to a very high mountain and showed him all the kingdoms of the world and their splendor. "All this I will give you," he said, "if you will bow down and worship me." Jesus said to him, "Away from me, Satan! For it is written: 'Worship the Lord your God, and serve him only.'" Then the devil left him, and angels came and attended him. (Matt. 4:8-11)

The devil is still trying to pull on Jesus' ego. "Hey, you can avoid the suffering ahead of you and still have it all; just worship me." It's a temptation you'll face often. You can have what you want by cutting corners. You don't have to do things God's way. Do what you have to do to get ahead. On your own. "Don't feel good? Try this ... this will make you feel better, won't it? God wants you happy."

Lies. Lies. Lies. That's all that the devil has to offer. So if the devil knows the Bible and has more experience than you, how do you beat him?

Know your Bible. The devil's a liar, and the truth of God's Word always wins. Read the Bible. Study the Bible. Memorize the Bible. The more of the Bible you know, the easier it is to know when your enemy is twisting it to trick you.

Stay connected to God. Jesus has an intimate relationship with His Father. When you're walking close to Jesus Christ, the devil doesn't stand a chance. "*Submit yourselves, then, to God. Resist the devil, and he will flee from you*" (James 4:7).

The final victory is with God. As you obey Christ, you lay hold of the promise that the day will soon come when the God of peace will crush the devil under your feet (Rom. 16:20).

10

Push
the Call Button

Help is One Call Away

My cousin Isabel was only nineteen when she found out that she had cancer of the lymph nodes. The whole family was shocked. So sweet, so young. We didn't see it coming. She was supposed to have her whole life ahead of her. What do you do? Many in our family are followers of Jesus. Within minutes of hearing the terrible news, we began to pray. The family prayed. Friends at church prayed. As I traveled to speak, I asked the crowds to add my cousin to their prayer lists.

Turbulence is a fact of life. Trouble will come in all shapes and sizes – many times when you least expect it. The analogy of the Christian experience being similar to a plane ride does break down, but consider this picture: We're all in this together. We're connected. When the plane shakes, everyone shakes. When it lands, everyone's made it home.

The captain, even though you can't see him, is traveling with you. During rough times it's good to remember that.

Jesus promised, "I am with you always, to the very end of the age" (Matt. 28:20). He is there. He's given His followers His Holy Spirit to live in them. He's not far away. Remember how the apostle Paul recounted his trouble in the last chapter? He was under such great pressure and trouble that he "felt the sentence of death." As Paul reflects on why this is happening to him, he says,

> But this happened that we might not rely on ourselves but on God, who raises the dead. He has delivered us from such a deadly peril, and he will deliver us. On him we have set our hope that he will continue to deliver us, as you help us by your prayers. Then many will give thanks on our behalf for the gracious favor granted us in answer to the prayers of many. (2 Cor. 1:9-11)

Paul feels like he's going to die if he doesn't get out of his mess. And he asks his friends to pray for him. Part of his safety, part of his escape from trouble, is wrapped up in his friends praying for him.

What is prayer? Simply put, prayer is personal communication with God. When you're flying, the captain is in the plane with you. You're not alone on the journey. And in our case, Jesus isn't too busy flying the plane to listen!

On a plane, there's a call button over your seat. If you need help, you press the button and one of the staff comes to your seat and asks, "How may I help you?"

What a great picture! Paul's in trouble and he tells his crew, "Push the button, man! Call out to God for us. We need God's help, and fast!"

The good news is that when we pray, we're not surprising God. Jesus said that *"your Father knows what you need before you ask him"* (Matt. 6:8).

God knows. So why bother praying? Because of what prayer does for us. Look at Jesus' clearest statements about prayer:

> This, then, is how you should pray: Our Father in heaven, hallowed be your name, your kingdom come, your will be done on earth as it is in heaven. Give us today our daily bread. Forgive us our debts, as we also have forgiven our debtors. And lead us not into temptation, but deliver us from the evil one. (Matt. 6:9-13)

Often called the Lord's Prayer, this prayer is really a great pattern for our communication with God. Notice the start: "Our Father in heaven." When I come to God with what's going on in my life, it brings me back to my dependence on Him to get me through. God is my Father. He's not far off in the distance and unknowable. Yes, He's the God of heaven. He made all things and holds the world in His hand. There's none like our God.

But He's *my* Father. He's my *Father*. Knowing God revolves around a relationship, not empty rituals. Jesus isn't saying that when you pray you have to quote this exact formula to get what you need. I often pray the Lord's Prayer, but it's not a hocus-pocus, here-you-go recipe.

It's about relationship. God wants us to come to Him, again and again, and be reminded that we should trust Him. We can trust Him. He's here for us. Praying makes that truth a reality.

Does Prayer Really Work?

Remember, God already knows what we need before we ask. Yet, the Bible tells us,

> You do not have, because you do not ask God. When you ask, you do not receive, because you ask with wrong motives, that you may spend what you get on your pleasures. (James 4:2-3)

God knows it all and you can't trick Him. Look at the next section of the Lord's Prayer: *"your kingdom come, your will be done on earth as it is in heaven."*

Ask. Ask often. Ask about everything you can think of. God wants you to come to Him with everything, to let Him know that you're depending on Him.

Sometimes we don't have because we don't ask! Jesus said,

> Ask and it will be given to you; seek and you will find; knock and the door will be opened to you. For everyone who asks receives; he who seeks finds; and to him who knocks, the door will be opened. (Matt. 7:7-8)

Don't be afraid to ask for too much. God has more than enough for all that you need. *Need*. That's the key. James wrote that when we pray, we need to keep our motives in check. Praying for selfish things is a waste of time. God knows what's best for us and He knows what to keep from us – for our own good.

And don't back away from persistence. There's something great about coming to God for a long time without getting an obvious answer. It keeps your focus on what God wants. Carmen and I prayed for years to have children. We were married for nine years before Jonah showed up. We asked. We asked again. We had hundreds of friends praying with us. I couldn't figure out for the life of me why we couldn't have children. Medical tests failed to indicate a problem – there was nothing wrong with either of us. But still no children. "God, do You want us to serve You without a family? You know how desperately we want to have children of our own. Do You want us to adopt? God, I don't understand."

Even when you hear silence, God is working behind the scenes. I'll never forget coming home from a long trip to England. Climbing upstairs completely exhausted, I opened our bathroom door to find a room dotted with balloons and a message written in lipstick on the mirror: "Welcome home, Daddy!"

Carmen was pregnant!

God provided at the right time. It wasn't my timing. But in essence we were praying the Lord's Prayer, *"your kingdom come, your will be done on earth as it is in heaven."* Hear me clearly – your prayers do make a difference.

Prayer doesn't change God's character. He's loving, kind, and good all of the time. But prayer may affect God's timing. There are examples in the Bible of God doing something quickly in response to believing prayer.

Speaking of timing – after we had Jonah, we started praying for another child. Three days before writing this chapter, I came home from another trip (notice the pattern) to find out that number two is on the way! God gave us a beautiful girl, Alina Gabrielle.

Another reminder that God is trustworthy. We asked. God provided ... beautifully!

> This is the confidence we have in approaching God: that
> if we ask anything according to his will, he hears us. And
> if we know that he hears us – whatever we ask – we know
> that we have what we asked of him. (1 John 5:14-15)

Practical note: Knowing your Bible not only gives you ammo to fight Satan's attacks, but also enhances your prayer life. Oftentimes I'll pray a part of the Bible. When I don't know what to do and I need direction, I'll pray James 1:5, *"If any of you lacks wisdom, he should ask God, who gives generously to all without finding fault."* When I'm in need of some specific thing (usually cash), I'll pray the Lord's Prayer, *"Give us today our daily bread."*

No magic formulas. God already knows what you need. Yet He wants you to express your heartfelt trust in Him and His love for you.

Side note: Notice the pronouns Jesus uses in His pattern for prayer – us, we, our. Prayer is personal. It's great to get alone with God and communicate with Him. But there is real power when followers of Jesus pray together. I unashamedly ask my friends to pray for and with me. As a matter of fact, some of my most meaningful times in prayer have been with my closest friends. Pray alone. Pray in groups. Just pray! Getting back to the Lord's Prayer: *"Forgive us our debts, as we also have forgiven our debtors."*

Want your prayers answered? Live in obedience to God. Disobedience, or sin, destroys. It pushes you away from a close relationship with God. When you pray, make sure that you spend time asking God for His forgiveness and to help you forgive others.

God wants you to be free. Holding things against other

people will only eat you alive. God, in Jesus Christ, has forgiven you – even though you don't deserve it – and He calls you to let go of grudges and past hurts. Holding on to a grudge doesn't change the other person, but it does fill your own heart with anger and bitterness, which harms your relationship with God. As you pray, ask God to reveal to you people whom you need to forgive.

It won't be easy.

I remember being hurt by a church leader in my junior year of high school. He said things about me and my family that were not true. I thought that he was a crook, a liar, and a fraud. I would pray each night that God would show other people who this guy really was. Every time I saw him, my anger grew. "How can that two-faced hypocrite pray and teach the Bible?"

I hated him.

Hate is like acid. The more you hold it, the deeper it burns. It wasn't affecting the other guy, but it was killing me. Praying one day, I was confronted by the Lord's Prayer and immediately this church leader came to mind. "Forgive us, as we have been forgiven."

Man, it was hard. I was in the right. He was clearly wrong. "God, will You help me forgive him? I'm sorry for holding this against him. You've forgiven me of so many stupid things. I leave him in Your hands."

I still didn't like him. But I started praying that God would bless and strengthen him. In time, I didn't feel the pain of his misguided words. It was in the past.

Years later I bumped into that man on the street. I knew the right thing to do. "Years ago," I said to him, "you said a few things about me and my family that I don't believe were true. I held it against you for a long time. I just wanted to say that I'm sorry for holding a grudge against you. Will you forgive me?"

> For if you forgive men when they sin against you, your heavenly Father will also forgive you (Matt. 6:14)

Finally, Jesus said, *"Lead us not into temptation, but deliver us from the evil one."*

God knows the past, present, and future. Remember, prayer is personal communication with God. It's about talking to Him ... and listening to Him. It's a two-way street. The ultimate goal of prayer is God's leadership. When I pray, I'm asking God to lead me away from sin, temptation, and evil and keep me close to Him. I ask God to keep me on the right path. He already wants to.

When I ask God to lead me, I'm often looking for His leadership. When I don't ask, I get sloppy. It's easy to go a day, a week, a month without meaningful prayer time. I've been there. And it leaves you empty. Make it a part of every day. You'll see the benefits in no time.

One last word about prayer: God doesn't always seem to answer, at least not in the way we hoped. Sometimes He clearly says "No." Other times it's "Yes, but not now." Sometimes it seems that He's not listening. Hang in there. God is Father to all who trust in Jesus Christ. It's about relationship. He's working out His plans, even though we don't often see any evidence.

My cousin's cancer continued to grow. Isabel had moments of relief, but the cancer spread and she eventually died. With hundreds praying for her healing, God didn't answer the way we wanted.

I don't know why God didn't heal my cousin. But I do

know this: God is trustworthy – He always knows best. And so I continue to pray.

Your kingdom come, your will be done on earth as it is in heaven.

11

Making the Most of the Journey

Discovering Your Life's Purpose

"Well, it's time for a little party."

That's the first thing I heard from the guy in the aisle seat next to me. I got stuck with a middle seat on a flight from Atlanta to Panama City, Panama. The last thing I wanted to do was talk. I had my iPod and a good book. The next few days in Panama would be slammed with meetings, and I needed some rest.

Still, I couldn't help but notice that my companion had turned straight to the back of the in-flight magazine to the page that listed available drinks.

"Hmm, I've never tried this Scotch before," he said out loud.

I'm thinking, *This is going to be a long flight.* Fortunately, the passenger in the window seat, an older man, was quietly writing on a notepad.

Ten minutes into the flight, Party Guy started ordering drinks – a few beers, a few Scotch on the rocks – and flipped through a golf magazine.

I pulled out my book, stuck the headphones on, and was happy to tune out ... until I felt a tap on the shoulder.

"Couldn't help but notice your book on God," Party Guy blurted. "That's a good thing."

I was expecting a sarcastic remark, even a debate about to unfold.

"Hi. I'm Lance."

"I'm Jose. Nice to meet you."

"So, what are doing in Panama?"

"I'm going to meet with pastors about an upcoming music festival ... a Christian music festival."

"That's great."

"And what are you headed down for?"

"A golf tournament."

Consumed by Golf

Turns out that Lance was a professional golfer kicking off the season in Panama City. My curiosity led me to ask, "Do pro golfers really read golf magazines?" They do, Lance told me, just to keep up on what people are saying about them!

We talked nonstop for the rest of the six-hour flight. Once Lance found out I was a preacher, our conversation quickly jumped to spiritual things.

Lance grew up hearing about God. His parents went to church and so did he for a while. It's what you did on Sunday in his southern town.

By the time he was ten he knew he'd turn pro. Winning tournament after tournament, Lance stacked the trophies in his room. "My life has always been about golf," he said. I thought I heard a tinge of regret in his words.

When I met Lance en route to Panama he was 39 and a four-year veteran on the PGA tour. Never a top-ranked player, but consistent. "You'd be surprised what goes on behind the scenes, Jose," he confessed. My ears perked up.

After telling me stories of parties, women, victories, and defeats, the wrinkle in the corner of his eyes gave away his regret. Life had become predictable. Another tournament, another party.

That changed, he said, when he met a Christian woman. They fell in love and quickly married. A baby boy was added to the family two years later.

They were on a family vacation in Hershey, Pennsylvania, when Lance suddenly collapsed at a theme park. He thought he was having a heart attack or stroke, and with his family looking over him in panic he was sure he was going to die.

His life was turned around that day. For the first time in his life he began to seriously think about his relationship with God. With his wife's help and encouragement, Lance placed his trust in Jesus Christ to forgive and rescue him.

That was five years ago.

I couldn't help but ask, "What's happened since then?" Other than going to Fellowship of Christian Athletes meetings on the Tuesday of each tour, Lance had done little to nourish his faith. "Two steps forward, six steps back" is the way he put it. "A golfer needs to be working on Sundays" – the final day of a tournament. Good point.

"My life is consumed by golf. I think about it all of the time. My swing. The next tournament. And these days

I haven't been playing really well. It gets to you. I know that God has something for me. I just don't know what it is."

Lance is right. There are no "accidents" in God's design. He made everything. And everything has purpose, a reason for being.

Lance excused himself for a minute to use the restroom. The older man in the window seat looked at me and smiled. Evidently he'd been listening to our whole conversation.

"Hello, my name is Bill," he said. "Seems like God wanted you to talk to Lance."

Bill was headed to Panama on one of his many mission trips. You could see the sparkle in his eye as he talked about the remote tribe that he and a few friends had been visiting in recent years. A government official had warned them that this tribe wasn't friendly to visitors and had a history of violence.

That didn't faze Bill one bit. On his last trip, he spent a month in their village, building relationships and sharing experiences. Why?

"Jose, as far as I know, this tribe doesn't have the Bible in their language. There is no church. Few have ever heard about Jesus."

By now, Bill was talking with the passion of a teenager. He's sixty-seven years old. "I almost didn't make this trip. I've had some medical problems. See here – I'm writing everything down for my wife. She's not well enough to come with me, but she loves to read the details when I get back.

"My doctor cleared me to go. As long as God gives me strength, I'll keep going."

Lance returned to his seat and I introduced Bill. "Hey Bill, can you repeat what you just told me?"

"As long as God gives me strength, I'll keep taking these mission trips."

Bill had figured out what Lance was still grappling with. *What am I really here for?* Bill was retired from his job, but he didn't consider himself a retiree. He's on a mission for God.

Near the end of the flight, Lance told me, "You know, kids look up to me. I could be more vocal about what God has done in my life."

"That's a great place to start," I said. "Hey, the next time you win a tournament and get some press, use that opportunity to give credit to God."

Wouldn't you know it, Lance won the tournament that weekend – his first win in years.

Coincidence?

What does God have in store for you?

It's worth finding out. Take a look at the apostle Paul's discovery about how God works:

> As for you, you were dead in your transgressions and sins, in which you used to live when you followed the ways of this world and of the ruler of the kingdom of the air, the spirit who is now at work in those who are disobedient. All of us also lived among them at one time, gratifying the cravings of our sinful nature and following its desires and thoughts. Like the rest, we were by nature objects of wrath. But because of his great love for us, God, who is rich in mercy, made us alive with Christ, even when we were dead in transgressions – it is by grace you have been saved.

And God raised us up with Christ and seated us with him in the heavenly realms in Christ Jesus, in order that in the coming ages he might show the incomparable riches of his grace, expressed in his kindness to us in Christ Jesus.

For it is by grace you have been saved, through faith–and this not from yourselves, it is the gift of God–not by works so that no one can boast. For we are God's workmanship, created in Christ Jesus to do good works, which God prepared in advance for us to do. (Eph. 2:1-10)

I'm quoting this at length so that you don't miss the point. You and I didn't deserve God's gift of life and forgiveness. We were doomed. But God was merciful to us.

When you placed your trust in Jesus Christ to rescue you, when you believed, God changed you. Now you are God's handiwork. It may not look like it when you stare in the mirror. Your report card may be mediocre. But God has set you apart as His master project. In His eyes, you're going to be a masterpiece! You can't take credit for that. It was and will always be a gift. God gives you the gift of forgiveness and life when you trust Him. You simply receive it. That's it.

That's why no matter what God has in store for you, there's no room to brag. Jesus changes you the moment you believe. You have peace with God. You're completely forgiven. You will be with God forever because of God's gift.

But what do I do now? The answer is in the last sentence quoted: He has created us anew in Christ Jesus, so that we can do the good things He planned for us long ago. God planned to rescue you.

God has also planned "good things" for you to do. God made you a new person to accomplish those things. Why? Because He's God. And He loves to take broken people, put them back together, and make something beautiful of their lives.

Please don't miss the point. We should ask God what *He* wants us to do, but not because we owe Him something. Salvation is a gift. You can never pay back God, not even by working for Him the rest of your life. Our sin debt is just too big. We should do those "good things" because we're grateful to God for what He's done for us. Grateful people want to follow God's leadership.

Who knows what God has in store for you to accomplish? It may be huge, and everyone will know about it. But it will probably be subtle, and only a few will know what you do in the name of Jesus.

In the end, God gets all of the credit for what He does in and through us.

My Story

I've always been a loudmouth. Growing up, I was the family clown. Always telling a joke. Anything for a laugh. And I love to talk. My poor mom – I don't know how she put up with me. I would wake up yapping and wouldn't stop till my head hit the pillow. You could have called me the "high-strung" child. Too much energy with a big mouth – a dangerous combination.

I placed my trust in Jesus Christ when I was just seven years old. My parents had taught me about Jesus and we regularly attended a great church. Diana, a family friend and former Sunday school teacher, says that when I was eight years old I said that I would be a preacher someday.

I don't remember. But early on I had this gut sense that telling others about Jesus was what I was supposed to do. In the eighth grade I went to a Christian school. It's the only year I went to private school. And looking back, I see God's hand at work.

Dolores Whimple was my teacher. She had served as a missionary, and she always encouraged her students to be open to what God would have us do. It rubbed off on me. She talked about what God was doing in Africa, and our church was sending a team that summer to Africa. Don't ask me how it happened, but I remember sitting at my desk convinced that God wanted me to go to Africa as a missionary.

"Mom and Dad," I announced when I got home, "I'm leaving school and going to serve God in Africa." Mind you, I'd never been there. I didn't have any money. I obviously didn't have an education!

Thankfully my parents didn't squash my wild idea. "You know what, Jose? If God wants you to go to Africa, He will make it clear. But for now, why don't you finish the eighth grade?"

I had put Africa on the back burner when I first picked up a pair of drumsticks. My mom made us take music lessons. *Piano?* Nope. *Guitar?* Too complicated. I picked up a pair of drumsticks and never put them down.

In high school I would always keep a pair of sticks in my backpack, along with *Modern Drummer* magazine and drum catalogues. It's all I thought about. I played drums in school, at home, and at church.

If you would have asked me when I was fifteen, "What are you going to do when you graduate?" I would have told you that I was going to be a drummer in a Christian rock band, touring the world and telling people about Jesus.

The "telling people about Jesus" part hadn't changed. I had just dropped the idea of Africa for a drum set! By the time I turned sixteen, I started to speak during our concerts. Slowly but surely I saw myself doing more speaking than playing. The transition was a struggle for me. I had lived, breathed, and dreamed playing drums. Yet as I prayed and thought about it, I sensed God leading me to prepare myself as a speaker rather than a musician.

I talked to my parents about it. I spoke with other Christians who knew me well and whom I trusted. They saw the change in me and encouraged me to follow God's direction. It sounds trivial, but it was a tough decision for me. I had planned to go to music school and be a professional drummer. Yet the next thing you know, I was applying for schools to study the Bible.

There weren't any flashes from heaven or audible voices. God communicated His plan for me in small ways. First I had the desire to go to Africa. Then to become a drummer, followed by a shift from drumming to speaking. It's hard to describe, but something inside gave me peace about going in a certain direction.

You know what? I have been to Africa to share the Good News of Jesus. And from time to time I do get to play the drums. But most of my time is spent traveling throughout America and many parts of the world, speaking to audiences about how they can know Jesus Christ personally.

Discovering your God-given purpose involves the natural and the supernatural. Naturally, I have always been bent toward the "up-front" or "on-stage" stuff. I've always loved to speak to crowds and enjoyed meeting new people and going to new places.

God has wired me for what He wants me to do. And He's wired you naturally for something that's perfect for you.

Chances are that what God has for you lines up with your natural talents and gifts. It isn't always the case. Sometimes God wants to stretch us a bit and see if we'll trust Him in areas that we're weak in. But more often, your natural gifts and passions are a part of God's plan and purpose for you. Then there's the supernatural element. God will nudge you, in big and subtle ways, to lead you in the right direction. What often starts as a fuzzy screen gradually becomes clear. My life looks totally different from how I pictured it when I was in the eighth grade. But I look back and also see how, little by little, God sharpened my life's focus.

God does have "good things" planned out for you. That may mean getting married someday and raising kids to know who He is. It could be a career path. For some, it's the call to serve Jesus in a specific ministry: to pastor a church, serve as a missionary, teach in a school.

Your journey is unique, charted by God expressly for you. For some, God's plan seems like a straight line. For others, it's like a maze. God weaves the twists and turns into something beautiful.

Consumed by God

So what do I do? Sit around waiting for God to lay things out, or figure it out myself?

Look at what Jesus says:

Therefore I tell you, do not be anxious about your life, what you will eat or what you will drink, nor about your body, what you will put on. Is not life more than food, and the body more than clothing? Look at the birds of the air: they neither sow nor reap nor gather into barns, and yet your heavenly Father feeds them. Are you not of more value than they? And which of you by being anxious can add a single hour to his span of life? And why are you anxious about clothing? Consider the lilies of the field, how they grow: they neither toil nor spin, yet I tell you, even Solomon in all his glory was not arrayed like one of these. But if God so clothes the grass of the field, which today is alive and tomorrow is thrown into the oven, will he not much more clothe you, O you of little faith? Therefore do not be anxious, saying, "What shall we eat?" or "What shall we drink?" or "What shall we wear?" For the Gentiles seek after all these things, and your heavenly Father knows that you need them all. But seek first the kingdom of God and his righteousness, and all these things will be added to you. (Matt. 6:25-33 ESV)

Live for Him. Make it your goal to look for God's perspective in your decisions today, both big and small. And "don't worry." When you seek God today, He'll give you everything you need to honor Him and accomplish His plan today. Tomorrow do the same thing. In time, I'm sure you'll find a pattern. You don't have to be stressed out about how things are going to work out. God has given you today to accomplish His agenda. Now, I hope that you're around to read the rest of this book. I hope that you'll live for decades. But there's no promise of that. Today – that's what you've got. Seek God's direction today. And tomorrow. And the next day. Jesus tells you clearly that "your heavenly Father already knows all your needs" in advance.

Lance was caught up in his professional golfing career, worried about his golf game and his future. I hope that my short time together with Lance helped him see that there is joy and fulfillment when we keep our focus on God and His kingdom agenda.

Finding your life's purpose is an ongoing discovery. Let God lead you. And He'll do it!

12

More
Seats Available

Always Room

God will use anyone. He has a way of taking even the most unlikely individuals and transforming them into useful leaders. This lesson was fixed in my brain in the sixth grade. Our family had just moved to a new neighborhood in Staten Island, New York. Across the street from our house was a schoolyard where everyone played basketball. I loved to mix it up with the older students.

Jeff Moore lived just down the road. He was eighteen. I was eleven and my brother Miguel was twelve. It was the summer after Jeff's high school graduation. He was an all-city track star. Good-looking. Athletic. And the world before him. Don't ask me why Jeff hung out with us. Looking back, I wouldn't have hung out with us. Whatever his reason, Jeff became like a big brother that year.

On a steamy August day, still dripping from the basketball game, Jeff stopped at our house on his way home. I clearly remember standing in between our red picket fence and blue station wagon parked in the driveway.

Standing there we somehow struck up a spiritual conversation. Don't ask me how it started. Before you know it, two punks – my brother and I – were sharing our faith with Jeff. Two kids vs. a high-school graduate.

God was with us. As boldly and clearly as we knew how, we shared with Jeff how Jesus had changed our lives. And Jesus wanted to change him, too. That was our little message.

Before Jeff walked home, we asked him, "Jeff, what do you think? Are you ready for Jesus to change you?"

"I don't know," he replied, "but I'll go home and think about it." The conversation ended with the sunset.

The next morning we had planned a trip to the community pool a few miles away. My parents wouldn't let us go without Jeff. The three of us splashed, swam, and escaped the blaring heat. It was great – for a while.

We went our separate ways to eat lunch. When we came back to the pool, Jeff found a few friends. Miguel and I did our own thing.

An hour or so later, I could see a commotion at the other end of the pool. The lifeguards were pulling some-one out of the water. Running over to get a closer look, I couldn't believe it. It was Jeff.

This had to be a joke. I was waiting for him to jump up and make everyone scream. Instead I stood by and watched the lifeguards pump on his chest and try mouth-to-mouth time and again.

Twenty minutes passed before the paramedics came. Jeff was pronounced dead on the spot. We watched our friend die. He went on to eternity right before our tender eyes.

After days of tears it dawned on us. The night before Jeff went on to eternity, God opened the door for my brother and me to share the Good News of Jesus. Did Jeff respond in trust? I hope, but I don't know.

None of Your Business

The followers of Jesus were shocked at His crucifixion. It's not what they were expecting. Even though Jesus had warned them of when and how He would die, they thought that Jesus was going to take over politically. They were expecting a victory, not a funeral.

As He had promised, Jesus rose again three days later.

After his suffering, he showed himself to these men and gave many convincing proofs that he was alive. He appeared to them over a period of forty days and spoke about the kingdom of God. On one occasion, while he was eating with them, he gave them this command: "Do not leave Jerusalem, but wait for the gift my Father promised, which you have heard me speak about. For John baptized with water, but in a few days you will be baptized with the Holy Spirit."

So when they met together, they asked him, "Lord, are you at this time going to restore the kingdom to Israel?" He said to them: "It is not for you to know the times or dates the Father has set by his own authority." (Acts 1:3-7)

These followers saw Jesus in person. He talked, ate, and hung out with them. And His message was focused on the "kingdom of God." God's work was on Jesus' mind. Now that sin had been paid in full, how was this message going to be spread to the nations?

Jesus was ready to pass on their new life's mission. Before that time they were only listeners. Now Jesus was sending them out as leaders – messengers of the good news. These followers had no idea of what was about to happen. So they asked Jesus, "Are you going to kick out the Romans and give this land back to the Jews?" It was an honest question. The Jews expected that their Rescuer – the Messiah – would restore the Jewish nation. But Jesus' agenda went beyond land and politics. He was going for hearts! "Lord, when are you going to fix things?" they asked. None of your business, indicated Jesus firmly. God has the timing firmed up, He told them. God is never surprised. When and how God does what He does shouldn't be our primary concern.

What does God want you to do with your life? Good question.

You can be confident of this: If you've trusted Jesus to rescue and lead you, then the dates and times are already in place.

Follow Jesus and He will lead you to do all that He's prepared. It's a freeing thought! While I should study, work hard, and prepare myself, what God wants me to do is in His hands. If I keep asking, in time He'll make it clear.

Power Tools

I grew up in New York City. We had a small lawn for a few years, but I don't know a thing about gardening or stuff like that. If you're looking for a great pizzeria, that I can help you with.

Carmen and I bought our first home several years ago, and the front yard was covered with bark dust. After two years of looking at the nasty stuff, my wife decided that it would be nice to have some grass to walk on. I don't blame her for asking, but I just didn't know how to fix it. I took out a rake and scraped off the bark dust. So far, so good. Then I used a shovel to move around the dirt and level the ground. I wasn't planting seeds; I was going for the "roll-a-lawn." I figured, flatten it out and throw rolls of sod. Instant lawn!

My neighbor looked out the window and said, "Jose, what are you doing?"

"Hey, I'm putting in a lawn."

"Aren't you going to till the soil?"

"What the soil?"

"Till it. You've got to turn the dirt over if the sod is going to grow any roots."

"Well, how do I that?"

"Go to Home Depot and rent a rototiller."

So away I go to Home Depot to rent a rototiller. Mind you, we've got this small front and back yard, but I come home with the biggest rototiller they've got. The guy who rented it to me told me that it's pretty simple to use. "Pull the cord to start it. When the engine's running, press the handle and it will do the job for you."

Sounded simple enough. I got to my front yard, pulled the cord, and the engine roared. I grabbed the handle and this thing took off. It yanked me across our little yard. I almost killed myself with this beast.

Power. It would have taken me hours to finish the job with a shovel. With a rototiller, it took me 10 minutes. I ended up doing the back yard and wanted to do the whole neighborhood.

I was now out of control. Thank God for a wife who told me to take that machine back. Nobody had told me how much easier it would be with this power tool.

That's really what Jesus was promising His followers – a power tool. He gave them a command:

> All authority in heaven and on earth has been given to me. Therefore go and make disciples of all nations, baptizing them in the name of the Father and of the Son and of the Holy Spirit, and teaching them to obey everything I have commanded you. And surely I am with you always, to the very end of the age. (Matt. 28:18-20)

But how would a few people take on a task that huge?

Power-filled Lives

Power. Jesus promised His followers power to live, and the power to take the message of forgiveness to everyone, everywhere.

I can't tell you specifically what God has for your life. But I'm confident of this: When God rescues you, you receive His Holy Spirit. And the Holy Spirit wants to give you the power to witness.

> "But you will receive power when the Holy Spirit comes on you; and you will be my witnesses in Jerusalem, and in all Judea and Samaria, and to the ends of the earth." After he said this, he was taken up before their very eyes, and a cloud hid him from their sight. (Acts 1:8-9)

How did the message of Jesus spread? Through this small group of followers – uneducated, ordinary men and women who trusted Jesus and received the Holy Spirit. Jesus' plan was and is simple. The Holy Spirit will give the followers of Jesus the ability to share the good news with those people close to them, with their communities, throughout their countries, and with every culture. That's the whole "Jerusalem, Judea, Samaria, ends of the earth" thing.

That's exactly what happened to His group of followers. As they were praying, the Holy Spirit came upon them, and they shared with a curious crowd what they had seen and heard. Jesus died for sins, was buried, and rose again to rescue us. Jesus is alive and offers the gift of eternal life to those who will trust Him.

On the first day, 3,000 people trusted Jesus. Not a bad start. Read the rest of the Book of Acts and you'll see that the Good News of Jesus was spread to the known world in their lifetime.

It happened in their generation, and it can happen in ours. What's it going to take? Obedience to God's clear command. Jesus told us that we would be witnesses for Him. If you've experienced God's forgiveness, you have something to share. You have a "testimony." You can share what you've seen and heard. You may not know it all, but you don't have to.

Love, not Guilt

God is not trying to set us up for failure. I remember going door-to-door in New York City as a teenager, sharing my testimony with all who would listen. Most didn't. Few people gave an immediate "yes" to the good news.

If that's the kind of response we get, why keep going out? Love. When you realize all that God has done for you, you start to see people differently – like God sees them. Lost and in need of help.

> For Christ's love compels us, because we are convinced that one died for all, and therefore all died. And he died for all, that those who live should no longer live for themselves but for him who died for them and was raised again. So from now on we regard no one from a worldly point of view. (2 Cor. 5:14-16)

It's easier to sit back and keep your relationship with God to yourself. Most of us have to be stirred to get beyond our comfort zones. Since Jesus died to save us, and when we trusted in Him we died to our own way of living, we should no longer live for ourselves, but for Jesus.

End result – we see people differently. It's not an "I'm better than you" attitude. It's not an "I've got it all together and know what's best for you" point of view. It's not even an "I'm right and you're wrong" point of view, although in Jesus we do know the truth. It's more like a "Man, you've got to know how good God is!" point of view.

That's what's happened to my brother Rafael. He has always worked out at a gym. After trusting in Jesus, he joined a church that runs a gym. The church owns the gym, but people from the community use it. He took a part-time job there for three reasons: First, he likes to work out. Second, it's a chance to serve. He's not a preacher (yet). He's more private about personal things than most. But by helping people, he's actively looking for a chance to serve. It could be as simple as teaching an exercise or offering a towel. Third, it's his best place to be a witness. People strike up a conversation and it's easy to share his story. Since he's fairly new, people ask how he got connected with the gym. "Let me tell you," he says. "A year ago I would never have thought that I'd be at a church. But ..." Rafael is respectful. He's polite. But he's also honest. Building relationships with the customers at the gym has led to spiritual conversations. Rafael's a witness.

Our Message

What do I say? If the door opens for me to talk about Jesus, what do I tell people?

The apostle Paul reminded a group in the city of Corinth about the heart of our message:

> For what I received I passed on to you as of first importance: that Christ died for our sins according to the Scriptures, that he was buried, that he was raised on the third day according to the Scriptures, and that he appeared to Peter, and then to the Twelve. (1 Cor. 15:3-5)

What is the gospel, the good news? Christ died for our sins and rose again. That's the truth of God's message in one sentence. Jesus died, according to the Scriptures. The whole Bible points to that one event. Jesus rose again, according to the Scriptures. This was no accident. It was God's proof to us that He can and will raise us up too. If God accepted Jesus and brought Him to life, then God will take a spiritually dead sinner like me and give me eternal life.

My good friend Greg Stier put together an acronym to help remember and clearly explain the gospel message. I'm sure you'll find it helpful.

The Gospel Journey

G God created us to be with Him (Gen. 1–2).

O Our sins separated us from God (Gen. 3).

S Sins cannot be removed by good deeds (Gen. 4 through Mal. 4).

P Paying the price for sin, Jesus died and rose again (Matthew through Luke).

E Everyone who trusts in Him alone has eternal life (John through Jude).

L Life with Jesus starts now and lasts forever (Rev.).

The content doesn't change. It's not my message; it's God's. The fun part is taking what God has done and explaining it in my own words.

What happened when I realized that I was created to know God? When did I realize that I was a sinner and separated from His love? When I found out that Jesus paid my penalty for sin, how did I respond? What difference has trusting in Jesus Christ made in my life?

Filling the Seats

I've flown on Singapore Airlines only once, on a flight from San Francisco to Chennai, India. It had to be one of the longest but most enjoyable flights I've ever taken. When people ask me what's the best airline I've flown, hands down I tell them "Singapore Airlines."

I'm not on the company's payroll, but I have sent a ton of business their way.

Why? The experience was great. Comfortable seats. Good food. Unbeatable service. Singapore Airlines is so good I want everyone to know about it.

I'm a satisfied customer and not ashamed to say it. God satisfies. He – not us – calls people to follow Him. God – not us – paid the price to rescue them. God wants to rescue everyone who will trust Him. Those are facts. But for some crazy reason God has entrusted you and me with telling others His message.

Bottom line: Others won't hear until we tell them.

> He has committed to us the message of reconciliation. We are therefore Christ's ambassadors, as though God were making his appeal through us. (2 Cor. 5:19-20)

There are empty seats on this plane. You're on board, so you're a witness. You've been given God's power to live the good news and share it. You don't have to do it in your own power. Forget the shovel. Grab on to the rototiller and watch God work!

(If you've never thought through how to share your testimony with others, turn the page for an easy exercise.)

My Testimony
Use this outline to plan your testimony. Under each of the main points, list the most important things that you want others to know about your life and your relationship with God. Organizing your testimony will help you share your story with other people.

I. What my life was like before I put my trust in Jesus.

_____
_____
_____
_____
_____
_____
_____

II. How I put my trust in Jesus.

_____
_____
_____
_____
_____
_____
_____
_____
_____

III. What my life is like since I put my trust in Jesus.

_____
_____
_____
_____
_____
_____
_____

13

Prepare for Landing

Journeys Are About Destinations

Killing time on a long flight, I picked up the in-flight magazine. "Three Perfect Days in Jamaica" – the perfect title for any passenger flying to cold Chicago. The article was only six pages long with lots of pictures. Forget the article. Just the pictures got me thinking I must be on the wrong flight. Jamaica, a tropical paradise. I've never been there, but those eyewitness accounts whet my appetite for more.

Jesus told His disciples,

> Do not let your hearts be troubled. Trust in God; trust also in me. In my Father's house are many rooms; if it were not so, I would have told you. I am going there to prepare a place for you. And if I go and prepare a place for you, I will come back and take you to be with me that you also may be where I am. You know the way to the place where I am going. (John 14:1-4)

What's heaven going to be like? I mean, are there big houses or what? Audio Adrenaline gave it a shot in their song "Big House."

Come, and go with me, to my Father's house.

Come, and go with me, to my Father's house.

It's a big, big house, with lots and lots of room,

A big, big table, with lots and lots of food,

A big, big yard, where we can play football,

A big, big house, it's my Father's house.

It's a fun song that adds to centuries-long speculation of what heaven is like. Football in the yard? I don't know. Although the Bible gives us enough information about heaven to convince us that we want to be there, the details are sketchy.

Ultimately, talking about heaven is really talking about hope.

Life on earth may feel like hell, but Jesus has promised us a better place. If you're living a comfortable life in America, then all of this heaven talk can seem like a crutch. Things are pretty good here. Why bother talking about the afterlife? I was visiting a remote tribe in northern Uganda. If you ever wanted to know where the end of the earth is, I may have stumbled on it. No one else for miles.

I was driven to a small church, with a hundred or so children sitting in the shade of a few trees planted near the building. I planned to share the Good News of Jesus, but I learned a lesson that morning – heaven is about hope. I got out of the car to hear these precious kids singing that Audio Adrenaline song! "Come, and go with me, to my Father's house." They sang their little hearts out and did the cutest hand motions to show how great heaven must be. Children with nothing. Rags for clothes. Little hope for an education. But overflowing with hope. Many of those children placed their trust in Jesus Christ that morning. Right there, in the middle of oblivion, they laid hold of God's promise – heaven.

Next Stop: Eternity

When will you face eternity? It's a trick question. Only the Father knows the day and the hour. Like my friend Jeff Moore, none of us knows exactly when we'll leave this earth for the Real World. There are really only two options: You'll die, or Jesus will return.

Having faced the real possibility of death a few times, I can tell you that the promise of heaven gives tangible hope. On the flight that made an emergency landing in Maine, I had enough time to think about my life. A good twenty minutes passed from the time the captain told us about the mechanical problems until the moment we landed.

Twenty minutes to think about the end. The reality is I was not afraid. I thought about my last words to Carmen. We weren't parents yet, and so I thought about the fact that she wanted to have my children – something we'd talked about for years.

At that moment, I felt sadness in my heart, but I had God's peace, too. I knew that Jesus Christ had removed my sin and that His promises are true. Heaven was a few steps away. I was ready.

Look at the promise to those who die trusting in Jesus:

> Brothers, we do not want you to be ignorant about those who fall asleep [die], or to grieve like the rest of men, who have no hope. We believe that Jesus died and rose again and so we believe that God will bring with Jesus those who have fallen asleep [died] in him. (1 Thess. 4:13-14)

The follower of Jesus has nothing to worry about. The same God who rescues us from sin will bring us to His eternal home

> If we live, we live to the Lord; and if we die, we die to the Lord. So, whether we live or die, we belong to the Lord. (Rom. 14:8)

I want to live a long life. I hope to hit triple digits. There are so many things that I want to see and do. But whether God lets me break 100 or I don't get another week, the end result is the same. I'll be with Jesus.

> Just as man is destined to die once, and after that to face judgment, so Christ was sacrificed once to take away the sins of many people. (Heb. 9:27-28)

There are no second chances; there is no second time around. When I die, I will go on to be judged by Jesus.

Jesus Will Return
The other option is that I'll still be alive when Jesus returns to the earth. When Jesus left the earth, the angels told His followers,

> This same Jesus, who has been taken from you into heaven, will come back in the same way you have seen him go into heaven. (Acts 1:11)

The first time Jesus came as a servant. He came in humility to rescue us. Now that He's paid that price, He'll return to judge.

Judge whom and what? Jesus makes a relationship with God possible. Anyone can receive His gift today. When Jesus returns, He will judge to see who received His gift and who rejected it.

> When the Son of Man comes in his glory, and all the angels with him, he will sit on his throne in heavenly glory. All the nations will be gathered before him, and he will separate the people one from another as a shepherd separates the sheep from the goats. He will put the sheep on his right and the goats on his left. Then the King will say to those on his right, "Come, you who are blessed by my Father; take your inheritance, the kingdom prepared for you since the creation of the world." (Matt. 25:31-34)

That's either an exciting or a frightening picture, depending on how you look at it. For some, it's a picture of future hope. When Jesus returns, He will gather us to live with Him. For those who reject Jesus now, it's a dark picture of doom. There will be no second chance, no "wait a minute, I trust You now" moments.

Whether you die and meet Jesus for judgment or He returns and takes you there, you will be judged. To those who trust in Jesus, a bright future awaits.

> And I heard a loud voice from the throne saying, "Now the dwelling of God is with men, and he will live with them. They will be his people, and God himself will be with them and be their God. He will wipe every

tear from their eyes. There will be no more death or mourning or crying or pain, for the old order of things has passed away." (Rev. 21:3-4)

And Now?

I can't tell you how big the houses are. Is heaven up or down or sideways from this planet? Who cares? It's a place where death does not exist. Crying is gone. Pain is in the past. In heaven, everything is new and will last forever. Heaven gives us hope and also helps us evaluate how we're living right now.

> But friends, that's exactly who we are: children of God. And that's only the beginning. Who knows how we'll end up! What we know is that when Christ is openly revealed, we'll see him – and in seeing him, become like him. All of us who look forward to his Coming stay ready, with the glistening purity of Jesus' life as a model for our own. (1 John 3:2-3 MSG)

If you are sure that you're going to heaven when you die, you ought to make the most of today. Why live below God's standards when He has so many wonderful things planned for you? Thinking about heaven reminds me that Jesus is worth serving, loving, and unashamedly obeying right now. Jesus is just that good.

Conclusion

Where

Are You Headed?

Decisions, Decisions, Decisions...

Lost. That's the best word to describe your life if you do not trust Jesus Christ. Lost now. And should you leave this planet without Jesus, you'll be lost – separated from God – forever. I hope this snapshot of what following Jesus looks like has stirred you to avoid hell and enter heaven by reaching out to Him and His ability to rescue you from your bad or stupid choices. I told you about my cousin Isabel who died so young. Getting cancer turned out to be the best thing that could have happened to her. As her condition turned for the worse, Isabel was confined to bed. Family would visit her every day to talk and pray.

One day my dad asked her, "Isabel, have you ever trusted Jesus Christ to save you?"

Isabel softly answered, "No."

Everyone was shocked. Surely Isabel was a Christian. She owned a Bible. She talked the lingo. She had gone to church every week since she was a little girl.

But she had never acknowledged her need for a Rescuer. Now she was running out of time.

So, as the Holy Spirit says:

> Today, if you hear his voice, do not harden your hearts. (Heb. 3:7-8)

Isabel placed her trust in Jesus Christ. Two weeks later she met Jesus in heaven. Life. Eternal life. That's God's offer to you today – right now. If God is stirring your mind and soul, convincing you that Jesus is who He says He is, then why not place your trust in Him? You don't have to go to a church building or, as I did, talk to a counselor on the telephone. Isabel was on her bed. You can make that decision right now, wherever you are. Ask God to rescue you. Transfer your trust from yourself to Jesus Christ.

It helps to pray – to verbalize your heartfelt belief. So if you're ready, you can pray something like this:

"God. I'm a mess. I'm a sinner. I come to You empty-handed.

"Jesus, I believe that You died and rose again to remove my sin. Forgive me. Accept me. I trust You to rescue me. Now Jesus, I put my life into Your hands. Lead me on. I'm Your follower. Thank You for rescuing me!"

Saying those words, or something like them, won't save you. But God knows your heart and sees your trust. Check out this awesome promise:

> I tell you the truth, whoever hears my word and believes him who sent me has eternal life and will not

be condemned; he has crossed over from death to life. (John 5:24)

You've crossed the line. You've boarded the plane. Your new life with God has just begun!

What Now?
Where are you on the journey? If you've placed your trust in Jesus Christ, have a question, or were touched by something in this book, take a minute and drop me an e-mail at airborne@josezayas.org. Yes, I read every one! I would love to know what God is doing in your life. Or you can write me at:

Jose Zayas
Post Office Box 1
Portland, OR 97207

We're on this journey together. Maybe we'll connect in an airport somewhere. You never know! (I'm the guy carrying too many bags, talking on his cell phone.) Until I see or hear from you, enjoy your time with Jesus . . . and get airborne for the ride of your life.

Peace,
Jose

About the Author

Jose Zayas lives to help people discover life in relationship with Jesus Christ. Using humor and everyday illustrations, he communicates the timeless truths of the Bible in today's language. Jose lives in Portland, Oregon, with his wife, Carmen, and two children.

Christian Focus Publications

publishes books for all ages

Our mission statement –

STAYING FAITHFUL

In dependence upon God we seek to impact the world through literature faithful to His infallible Word, the Bible. Our aim is to ensure that the Lord Jesus Christ is presented as the only hope to obtain forgiveness of sin, live a useful life and look forward to heaven with Him.

REACHING OUT

Christ's last command requires us to reach out to our world with His gospel. We seek to help fulfil that by publishing books that point people towards Jesus and help them develop a Christ-like maturity. We aim to equip all levels of readers for life, work, ministry and mission.

Books in our adult range are published in three imprints:

Christian Focus contains popular works including biographies, commentaries, basic doctrine and Christian living. Our children's books are also published in this imprint.

Mentor focuses on books written at a level suitable for Bible College and seminary students, pastors, and other serious readers. The imprint includes commentaries, doctrinal studies, examination of current issues and church history.

Christian Heritage contains classic writings from the past.

Christian Focus Publications Ltd,
Geanies House, Fearn, Ross-shire,
IV20 1TW, Scotland, United Kingdom
www.christianfocus.com